SORROW'S KITCHEN

THE LIFE AND FOLKLORE OF
ZORA NEALE HURSTON

MARY E. LYONS

Aladdin Paperbacks

Aladdin Paperbacks
An imprint of Simon & Schuster Children's Publishing Division
1230 Avenue of the Americas, New York, NY 10020
Text copyright © 1990 by Mary E. Lyons
All rights reserved including the right of reproduction
in whole or in part in any form.
Printed in the United States of America
10   9
A hardcover edition of *Sorrow's Kitchen* is available from Atheneum Books for Young Readers, Simon & Schuster Children's Publishing Division.

Library of Congress Cataloging-in-Publication Data
Lyons, Mary (Mary E.)
Sorrow's kitchen : the life and folklore of Zora Neale Hurston /
Mary E. Lyons.—1st Collier Books ed.
p.   cm.
Summary: Describes the life and work of the prolific black author who wrote stories, plays, essays, and articles, recorded black folklore, and was involved in the Harlem Renaissance.
ISBN 0-02-044445-1
1. Hurston, Zora Neale–Juvenile literature.   2. Novelists, American–20th century–Biography–Juvenile literature.   3. Folklorists–United States–Biography–Juvenile literature.   4. Afro-Americans–Biography–Juvenile literature.   [1. Hurston, Zora Neale.   2. Authors, American.
3. Afro-Americans–Biography.]   I. Title.
PS3515.U789Z78   1993
813'.52–dc20   [B]   92-30600

To my husband, Paul Collinge,
and my mother, Evelyn Lyons

I been in sorrow's kitchen
and I done licked the pots clean.

—Florida folk saying

PREFACE

Zora Neale Hurston was the author of seven books and over one hundred short stories, plays, essays, and articles. Called "a genius of the South" by Alice Walker, she wrote more than any black woman of her time. She was an important member of the Harlem Renaissance and the first black author to write a popular book of black folklore, *Mules and Men*. Two of her books are considered masterpieces: *Their Eyes Were Watching God* and *Moses, Man of the Mountain*.

Zora Hurston had a special talent for storytelling. She used her talent to create realistic black characters and speech in her books, an ability that delighted some critics and irritated others. Outrageous and funny, she also had a gift for making people laugh.

Her mother used to say that someone had put "travel dust" on the doorstep the day Zora was born. The dust must have worked, for Zora's thirty-year writing career took her from Florida to Baltimore, Washington, D.C., to New York City, Harlem to the Caribbean Islands, and back to New York. Finally, Zora returned to Florida, where she died alone and poor in 1960.

Once Zora said, "I love courage . . . I worship strength." Blessed with both qualities, she overcame hardship with humor to bring us books that entertain and enrich. To those who knew her when she was alive, and to those who meet her now through her stories, Zora Neale Hurston and her writing are unforgettable.

ACKNOWLEDGMENTS

Grateful acknowledgment is made for permission granted by the following publishers and authors' representatives to reprint selections.

"Courting Ritual" from *Mule Bone: A Comedy of Negro Life* by Langston Hughes and Zora Neale Hurston. Reprinted by permission of Harold Ober Associates and of the Zora Neale Hurston Estate.

"Mama's Child," "Wandering," and "Walking on Flypaper" from *Dust Tracks on a Road* by Zora Neale Hurston. Copyright 1942 by Zora Neale Hurston. Renewed 1970 by John C. Hurston. Reprinted by permission of Harper & Row, Publishers, Inc.

"The Eatonville Anthology" from *I Love Myself When I Am Laughing and Then Again When I Am Looking Mean and Impressive* by Zora Neale Hurston. Published with permission of the Zora Neale Hurston Estate.

"Mosquito Lies" and "Black Cat Bone" from *Mules and Men* by Zora Neale Hurston. Copyright 1935 by Zora Neale Hurston. Renewed 1963 by John C. Hurston. Reprinted by permission of Harper & Row, Publishers, Inc.

"Horse Bath and Bitters" and "Zombies" from *Tell My Horse* by Zora Neale Hurston. Copyright 1938 by Zora Neale Hurston. Renewed 1966 by Joel Hurston and John C. Hurston. Reprinted by permission of Harper & Row, Publishers, Inc.

"Jealousy" from *Their Eyes Were Watching God* by Zora Neale Hurston. Copyright 1937 by Harper & Row, Publishers, Inc. Renewed 1965 by John C. Hurston and Joel Hurston. Reprinted by permission of Harper & Row, Publishers, Inc. and of Virago Press, Ltd.

"High John the Conquer" by Zora Neale Hurston. Published with permission of the Zora Neale Hurston Estate.

"Looking for Zora" from *In Search of Our Mothers' Gardens*. Copyright © 1975 by Alice Walker. Reprinted by permission of Harcourt Brace Jovanovich, Inc.

CONTENTS

◆ 1 ◆

HOME

Zora Neale Hurston did things her own way from the day she was born. On a cool January morning in 1891, she waited until the midwife was at a hog killing and her father was out of town. Then, eager to get started with life, she rushed into the world, "crying strong." Her mother had no choice in the matter and delivered Zora all alone. When a neighbor happened to stop by, he cut the cord, applied the bellyband, and Zora was on her independent way.

She was the seventh child in a family of eight—six boys and two girls. Her father, John Hurston, had a wandering eye for other women and spent months at a time away from home. Still, he was a skilled carpenter and a good provider. He was also a Baptist preacher and the town mayor. He wrote the town laws, including one that forbade pregnant dogs to roam the streets because they might shock the ladies.

John was the strongest man in the village of Eaton-

1

ville, Florida. Tall and heavily muscled, he could swing "bales of cotton like suitcases" and swim Lake Maitland from end to end. "No man," Zora remembered, "could put my father's shoulder to the ground."

To Zora, her father was invincible, despite their rocky relationship. From her earliest years, she felt unloved by him. According to Zora, he threatened to cut his throat when he heard another daughter had been born, for her older sister, Sarah, was already "Papa's girl-baby." Zora was quite jealous of the attention her sister received and admitted it made her into "a tiger."

As a result, she crossed her father when she could. He forbade her to read novels, considering them "works of the devil," but Zora read everything she could find. She eagerly devoured fairy tales, "blood and thunder" dime novels, Nick Carter detective books, even advertisements.

Her father also disapproved of poetry. One night at supper, eight-year-old Zora announced that she had written some poems. "I'm going to be a poet like Longfellow!" she said. John Hurston was horrified. He could preach like a poet, but he knew nothing about poetry.

"It is my understanding that poets are low-living creatures," he thundered, "with no God in their hearts and no Bible in their hands. If you want to do something, be a missionary!" Such arguments were frequent between Zora and Papa, and usually ended with a whipping or a chase out the kitchen door.

Lucy Hurston, Zora's mother, was the "hard-driving force" in the family. A country school teacher when she married at sixteen, she taught all the Hurston children to read and write. Zora could read before school age, and she later liked to boast that six of the eight children had earned college degrees.

Zora remembered a lot of whippings at home and school to "break my spirit." Mama spanked her for repeating gossip she had overheard from adults. And she got a licking when she sat on the gatepost and called to white travelers driving down the road, "Don't you want me to go a piece of the way with you?"

She was sassy and impudent, but it was clear to Lucy Hurston that Zora was also bright. Lucy was proud of her daughter's talents—Zora was "Mama's child." When she came home with wild stories about talking to birds and walking on the lake, Mama listened.

Zora's grandmother would "foam at the mouth" and accuse Zora of being a lying heifer. "You hear dat young'un stand up here and lie like dat?" she would

Hungerford School in Eatonville, Florida, around 1907. The school was established in 1889 on thirty-four acres of land. Zora Neale Hurston completed at least six grades in this school. *Courtesy town of Eatonville, Florida*

fuss. "And you ain't doing nothing to break her of it? Grab her! Stomp her guts out! Ruin her!"

"Oh, she's just playing," Mama would say in defense, letting Zora know she was free to keep talking to the pine trees and playing with the moon. Mama gave Zora's imagination room to grow, and it bloomed like the Cape jasmine bushes around their house. The fanciful stories she made up as a tiny girl were just the beginning of a lifetime of tales.

In "Mama's Child," Zora remembers the setting of her early childhood. She recalls the house her father built, the food she ate, and the games she played. She also describes the two most important people in her young life: Mama and Papa.

MAMA'S CHILD

We lived on a big piece of ground with two big chinaberry trees shading the front gate and Cape jasmine bushes with hundreds of blooms on either side of the walks. I loved the fleshy, white, fragrant blooms as a child but did not make too much of them. They were too common in my neighborhood. When I got to New York and found out that the people called them gardenias, and that the flowers cost a dollar each, I was impressed. The home folks laughed when I went back down there and told them. Some of the folks did not want to believe me. A dollar for a Cape jasmine bloom! Folks up north there must be crazy.

There were plenty of orange, grapefruit, tangerine, guavas and other fruits in our yard. We had a five-acre garden with things to eat growing in it, and so we were never hungry. We had chicken on the table often; home-cured meat, and all the eggs we wanted. It was a common thing for us smaller children to fill the iron tea-kettle full of eggs and boil them, and lay around in the yard and eat them until we were full. Any left-over boiled eggs could always be used for missiles. There was plenty of fish in the lakes around the town, and so we had all that we wanted. But beef stew was something rare. We were all very happy whenever Papa went to Orlando and brought back something delicious like stew-beef. Chicken and fish were too common with us. In the same way, we treasured an apple. We had oranges, tangerines and grapefruit to use as hand-grenades on the neighbors' children. But apples were something rare. They came from way up north.

Our house had eight rooms, and we called it a two-story house; but later on I learned it was really one story and a jump. The big boys all slept up there, and it was a good place to hide and shirk from sweeping off the front porch or raking up the back yard.

Downstairs in the dining-room there was an old "safe," a punched design in its tin doors. Glasses of guava jelly, quart jars of pear, peach and other kinds of preserves. The left-over cooked foods were on the lower shelves.

There were eight children in the family, and our

house was noisy from the time school turned out until bedtime. After supper we gathered in Mama's room, and everybody had to get their lessons for the next day. Mama carried us all past long division in arithmetic, and parsing sentences in grammar, by diagrams on the blackboard. That was as far as she had gone. Then the younger ones were turned over to my oldest brother, Bob, and Mama sat and saw to it that we paid attention. You had to keep on going over things until you did know. How I hated the multiplication tables—especially the sevens!

We had a big barn, and a stretch of ground well covered with Bermuda grass. So on moonlight nights, two-thirds of the village children from seven to eighteen would be playing hide and whoop, chick-mah-chick, hide and seek, and other boisterous games in our yard. Once or twice a year we might get permission to go and play at some other house. But that was most unusual. Mama contended that we had plenty of space to play in; plenty of things to play with; and, furthermore, plenty of us to keep each other's company. If she had her way, she meant to raise her children to stay at home. She said that there was no need for us to live like no-count Negroes and poor-white trash—too poor to sit in the house—had to come outdoors for any pleasure, or hang around somebody else's house. Any of her children who had any tendencies like that must have got it from the Hurston side. It certainly did not come from the

Pottses. Things like that gave me my first glimmering of the universal female gospel that all good traits and leanings come from the mother's side.

Mama exhorted her children at every opportunity to "jump at de sun." We might not land on the sun, but at least we would get off the ground. Papa did not feel so hopeful. Let well enough alone. It did not do for Negroes to have too much spirit. He was always threatening to break mine or kill me in the attempt. My mother was always standing between us. She conceded that I was impudent and given to talking back, but she didn't want to "squinch my spirit" too much for fear that I would turn out to be a mealy-mouthed rag doll by the time I got grown. Papa always flew hot when Mama said that. I do not know whether he feared for my future, with the tendency I had to stand and give battle, or that he felt a personal reference in Mama's observation. He predicted dire things for me. The white folks were not going to stand for it. I was going to be hung before I got grown. Somebody was going to blow me down for my sassy tongue. Mama was going to suck sorrow for not beating my temper out of me before it was too late. Posses with ropes and guns were going to drag me out sooner or later on account of that stiff neck I toted. I was going to tote a hungry belly by reason of my forward ways. My older sister was meek and mild. She would always get along. Why couldn't I be like her? Mama would keep right on with whatever she was doing and remark, "Zora is my young'un, and Sarah is yours. I'll be bound mine will come out more than conquer. You leave her alone. I'll tend to her when I figger she needs it." She meant by that that Sarah had a disposition like Papa's, while mine was like hers.

Behind Mama's rocking-chair was a good place to be in times like that. Papa was not going to hit Mama. He was two hundred pounds of bone and muscle and Mama weighed somewhere in the nineties. When people teased him about Mama being the boss, he would say he could break her of her headstrong ways if he wanted to, but she was so little that he couldn't find any place to hit her. My Uncle Jim, Mama's brother, used to always take exception to that. He maintained that if a woman had anything big enough to sit on, she had something big enough to hit on. That was his firm conviction, and he meant to hold on to it as long as the bottom end of his backbone pointed towards the ground—don't care who the woman was or what she looked like, or where she came from. Men like Papa who held to any other notion were just beating around the bush, dodging the issue, and otherwise looking like a fool at a funeral.

Papa used to shake his head at this and say, "What's de use of me taking my fist to a poor weakly thing like a woman? Anyhow, you got to submit yourself to 'em, so there ain't no use in beating on 'em and then have to go back and beg 'em pardon."

So Papa did not take Uncle Jim's philosophy

about handling the lady people too seriously. Every time Mama cornered him about some of his doings, he used to threaten to wring a chair over her head. She never even took enough notice of the threat to answer. She just went right on asking questions about his doings and then answering them herself until Papa slammed out of the house looking like he had been whipped all over with peach hickories. But I had better not let out a giggle at such times, or it would be just too bad.

Our house was a place where people came. Visiting preachers, Sunday school and B.Y.P.U. workers, and just friends. There was fried chicken for visitors, and other such hospitality as the house afforded.

Papa's bedroom was the guest-room. Store-bought towels would be taken out of the old round-topped trunk in Mama's room and draped on the washstand. The pitcher and bowl were scrubbed out before fresh water from the pump was put in for the use of the guest. Sweet soap was company soap. We knew that. Otherwise, Octagon laundry soap was used to keep us clean. Bleached-out meal sacks served the family for bath towels ordinarily, so that the store-bought towels could be nice and clean for visitors.

Company got the preference in toilet paper, too. Old newspapers were put out in the privy house for family use. But when company came, something better was offered them. Fair to middling guests got sheets out of the old Sears, Roebuck

catalogue. But Mama would sort over her old dress patterns when really fine company came, and the privy house was well scrubbed, lime thrown in, and the soft tissue paper pattern stuck on a nail inside the place for the comfort and pleasure of our guests.

◆ 2 ◆

EATONVILLE

Lucy Hurston told her daughter to be herself, behavior that came naturally to free-spirited Zora. It was also easier for her to be herself because she grew up in Eatonville, Florida. The small village of Eatonville was the first incorporated black community in America, with its own laws, town council, and mayor.

Eatonville residents were somewhat safe from lynchings and other racial violence, although Zora recalled that the village did its best to teach her to fear white strangers. With good reason—in 1896, the year she was five years old, there were seventy-seven lynchings in the United States, many of them in the rural south.

In that same year, the Supreme Court ruled that "separate but equal" facilities were constitutional. Discrimination against blacks was a fact of life throughout the country, including the North, but the new ruling now made segregation legally enforceable. Southern states and towns passed Jim Crow laws. These laws

11

An Eatonville church, painted by André Smith. A church was the first structure built in Eatonville. *Courtesy town of Eatonville, Florida*

made it possible to segregate public transportation, waiting rooms, restaurants, schools, and hospitals. Virtually any area where the races might mingle could be designated as "whites only."

Zora was sheltered from all this. In isolated Eatonville, there was no need for legalized segregation. Her early childhood was so free from discrimination that it took a trip to Jacksonville, with its segregated streetcars and "white people with funny ways," to make her know she was "a little colored girl." Away from the familiar whites around Eatonville, Zora sensed an immediate difference. There was no "sure sense of welcome" in Jacksonville, she recalled, no friendly piece of candy when she walked into a store.

Zora did get a piece of candy or a bag of crackers when she walked into her favorite place in Eatonville: Joe Clarke's store. The "heart and spring of the town," the store was just through the trees from her house. When Zora ran an errand for her mother, she waited around and listened to the adults until she heard Mama's voice calling her home with the sugar. On Joe Clarke's porch, Zora heard jokes, town gossip, and Bubber Mimms's blues guitar.

But it was the "lying" sessions that she loved most. Lying sessions (Who could tell the tallest tale?) introduced her to Brer Rabbit, Sister Snail, John the Conqueror, and other folk characters. The dozens of folktales she heard inspired her to make up her own stories, and Zora fashioned a cast of homemade dolls to star in imaginary dramas.

Miss Corn-Shuck had lovely corn-silk hair. She and Mr. Sweet Smell (a bar of Pear's soap filched from Mama's dresser drawer) wanted to be married by Reverend Door-Knob. But the wedding was not to be, for jealous Miss Corn-Cob always ruined the ceremony. She played a series of nasty tricks on the unlucky couple, from eating all the refreshments (a can of condensed milk) to pushing the reverend into the (washbasin) lake.

Zora's playmates stayed with her for years, taking

trips with her "to where the sky met the ground." She later remembered that one day they were simply gone, their creator too old to be "fit company for spirits." Like many authors who compose stories in their childhood, Zora's imaginary characters and elaborate plots foreshadowed an adult writing ability.

In some ways, Zora's Eatonville experiences were the most important of her life. Like a recurring dream, the memories of Eatonville emerge again and again in her writings. The folklore she heard as a child reappears in her book *Mules and Men*. The main characters in her first novel, *Jonah's Gourd Vine*, are patterned after John and Lucy Hurston. And in *Their Eyes Were Watching God*, she named a character after her favorite childhood food: stew beef.

Her family, the village people, and the tales on Joe Clarke's store porch instilled in Zora a deep respect for the folkways of her race. She spent a lifetime writing books that celebrate the black culture she lived as a child. For Zora, just as for a character in one of her books, "every day had a store in it."

In "Wandering," Zora remembers her mother's death, a tragedy that marked the end of her childhood. "Wandering" reveals how Zora could turn any experience into a story. Death becomes a folk figure who prowls the house with soft feet and square toes—an actual creature with human qualities.

Zora mentions some of the folk beliefs of her Eatonville childhood: A person will die easier if the pillow is removed before death. The mirror must be covered or it will always reflect the image of the deceased. If the dying person gazes upon an uncovered clock at the time

A street scene in Eatonville, painted by Bok Fellows. The old wooden buildings have since been replaced by colorful stucco houses. Eatonville celebrated its centennial in 1987, when it paid tribute to Zora with a play performed at the Hungerford School. *Courtesy town of Eatonville, Florida*

of death, the clock will stop forever. Eatonville folk believed that these measures kept the spirit of the dead from coming back to haunt the living.

WANDERING

I knew that Mama was sick. She kept getting thinner and thinner and her chest cold never got any better. Finally, she took to bed.

She had come home from Alabama that way. She had gone back to her old home to be with her sister during her sister's last illness. Aunt Dinky had lasted on for two months after Mama got there, and so Mama had stayed on till the last.

It was not long after Mama came home that she began to be less active. Then she took to bed. I knew she was ailing, but she was always frail, so I did not take it too much to heart. I was nine years old, and even though she had talked to me very earnestly one night, I could not conceive of Mama actually dying. She had talked of it many times.

That day, September 18th, she had called me and given me certain instructions. I was not to let them take the pillow from under her head until she was dead. The clock was not to be covered, nor the looking-glass. She trusted me to see to it that these things were not done. I promised her as solemnly as nine years could do, that I would see to it.

What years of agony that promise gave me! In the first place, I had no idea that it would be soon. But that same day near sundown I was called upon to set my will against my father, the village dames and village custom. I know now that I could not have succeeded.

I had left Mama and was playing outside for a little while when I noted a number of women going inside Mama's room and staying. It looked strange. So I went on in. Papa was standing at the foot of the bed looking down on my mother, who was breathing hard. As I crowded in, they lifted up the bed and turned it around so that Mama's eyes would face the east. I thought that she looked to me as the head of the bed was reversed. Her mouth was slightly open, but her breathing took up so much of her strength that she could not talk. But she looked at me, or so I felt, to speak for her. She depended on me for a voice.

The Master-Maker in His making had made Old Death. Made him with big, soft feet and square toes. Made him with a face that reflects the face of all things, but neither changes itself, nor is mirrored anywhere. Made the body of Death out of infinite hunger. Made a weapon for his hand to satisfy his needs. This was the morning of the day of the beginning of things.

But Death had no home and he knew it at once.

"And where shall I dwell in my dwelling?" Old Death asked, for he was already old when he was made.

"You shall build you a place close to the living, yet far out of the sight of eyes. Wherever there is a building, there you have your platform that comprehends the four roads of the winds. For your hunger, I give you the first and last taste of all things."

We had been born, so Death had had his first taste of us. We had built things, so he had his platform in our yard.

And now, Death stirred from his platform in his secret place in our yard, and came inside the house.

Somebody reached for the clock, while Mrs. Mattie Clarke put her hand to the pillow to take it away.

"Don't!" I cried out. "Don't take the pillow from

under Mama's head! She said she didn't want it moved!"

I made to stop Mrs. Mattie, but Papa pulled me away. Others were trying to silence me. I could see the huge drop of sweat collected in the hollow at Mama's elbow and it hurt me so. They were covering the clock and the mirror.

"Don't cover up that clock! Leave that looking-glass like it is! Lemme put Mama's pillow back where it was!"

But Papa held me tight and the others frowned me down. Mama was still rasping out the last morsel of her life. I think she was trying to say something, and I think she was trying to speak to me. What was she trying to tell me? What wouldn't I give to know! Perhaps she was telling me that it was better for the pillow to be moved so that she could die easy, as they said. Perhaps she was accusing me of weakness and failure in carrying out her last wish. I do not know. I shall never know.

Just then, Death finished his prowling through the house on his padded feet and entered the room. He bowed to Mama in his way, and she made her manners and left us to act out our ceremonies over unimportant things.

I was to agonize over that moment for years to come. In the midst of play, in wakeful moments after midnight, on the way home from parties, and even in the classroom during lectures. My thoughts would escape occasionally from their confines and stare me down.

Now, I know that I could not have had my way

against the world. The world we lived in required those acts. Anything else would have been sacrilege, and no nine-year-old voice was going to thwart them. My father was with the mores. He had restrained me physically from outraging the ceremonies established for the dying. If there is any consciousness after death, I hope that Mama knows that I did my best. She must know how I have suffered for my failure.

But life picked me up from the foot of Mama's bed, grief, self-despisement and all, and set my feet in strange ways. That moment was the end of a phase in my life. I was old before my time with grief of loss, of failure, and of remorse. No matter what the others did, my mother had put her trust in me. She had felt that I could and would carry out her wishes, and I had not. And then in that sunset time, I failed her. It seemed as she died that the sun went down on purpose to flee away from me.

That hour began my wanderings. Not so much in geography, but in time. Then not so much in time as in spirit.

Mama died at sundown and changed a world. That is, the world which had been built out of her body and her heart.

◆ 3 ◆
BALTIMORE AND WASHINGTON

Dark years followed Lucy Hurston's death. Since Papa was seldom at home, he sent Zora to boarding school in Jacksonville with her older brother, Bob, and her sister, Sarah. Two months later, homesick Sarah returned to Eatonville, only to find that her father had married a woman who would not tolerate her stepchildren. She insisted that Sarah move out and that Papa beat her with a buggy whip for commenting on their new marriage.

Zora was furious when she heard the news. She dreamed of revenge. "I wanted blood," she remembered, "and plenty of it." It would be six years before she could feel "flesh against flesh," but Zora would eventually even the score with her stepmother.

She stayed in Jacksonville for only one year. Under the influence of his new wife, Papa stopped sending payments for room and board. When the school year

20

ended, he wrote to say that the school could adopt her. They could not adopt her, of course, but the message was clear. Zora was an unwanted child.

The school bought her a ticket back to Eatonville, and Zora returned "to my father's house which was no longer home." The stepmother had her way, and the four youngest children, including Zora, were placed in the homes of friends and relatives. She described the next five years as "haunted."

While she yearned for "family love and peace and a resting place," Zora lived in a series of homes where she got hand-me-downs and hit-or-miss meals instead. She was expected to provide some money for her support, so despite her longing for books and school, she dropped out to work as a maid. Feeling "restless and unstable," Zora held many such jobs, but never for long. She found the work boring, and it depressed her to see others who were able to go to school.

Because she was deliberately misleading about her age, we don't know how long this period in Zora's life lasted. Census records indicate that she was born in 1891, but invariably she used different dates, ranging from 1898 to 1910. Her autobiography states that she was only nine when her mother died, but she was probably thirteen.

Zora's five haunted years were at least ten. Why did she choose to lie about her age? During this time, there may have been a secret marriage that she later wanted to conceal. As she grew older, perhaps it became advantageous to hide her true age—when seeing a younger man, for instance, or applying for school or a job. Whatever the reasons, the years after her mother's

In later years, Zora described herself as "extra strong," not afraid of getting hurt when she played with the boys. *Courtesy Library of Congress*

death were hard ones. "Poverty smells like death," she discovered. "People can be slave ships in shoes."

At her father's request, Zora eventually moved back home. But the reunion was short-lived. Within a month, she had a violent argument with her step-mother. Zora had a long memory, and she didn't miss this opportunity to settle the debt for the blows her sister had suffered six years earlier.

In a knockdown fistfight with scratching, clawing, and spitting, Zora threw a hatchet at the hated woman. Luckily, she missed. The fight ended when her step-mother slumped exhausted to the floor. Zora, the victor in battle, also won the war: John Hurston refused to have Zora arrested, and his second wife, "her lip hung down lower than a mason's apron," left him. The marriage ended in divorce.

Still wandering, Zora left home again. She moved to another town and then lived with her oldest brother. Finally, she left Florida, boarding a train with a suitcase filled with newspapers to keep her comb, brush, and toothpaste from rattling.

For a year and a half, she worked as a wardrobe girl for Miss M, an actress in a traveling light-opera show. The experience widened Zora's world. She had only been as far as Jacksonville, but now she would see the whole Southeast. Zora remembered being dazzled by the company's private coach car and the teasing affection of the members of the troupe—they joked, played games with her, and stuffed her with ice cream and Coca-Cola.

A naive young woman when she joined the troupe,

Zora left it "loosened up in every joint and expanded in every direction." As the train toured its way through the South, she borrowed books, listened to opera, and absorbed new ideas from the performers, including one that would influence her in years to come—she observed that a career could fill up "the empty holes left by love."

In Baltimore she left the troupe, determined to finish her education: "I took a firm grip on the only weapon I had—hope—and set my feet." Zora had an amazing capacity for making friends wherever she went. The friends she made in Baltimore helped her find a job and a home. Night school led her to Morgan Academy, where she started high school with one dress, one set of underwear, and one pair of shoes.

Zora was surrounded in class by attractive, well-dressed classmates. She immediately made friends. They were kind to her and gave her clothes, even down to a handkerchief. But it must have been hard when they teased, "Zora, what do you think you'll wear to school tomorrow?" Embarrassed by her appearance, she felt like her face "had been chopped out of a knot of pine wood with a hatchet. . . ."

Still, Zora was happy to be back in school. She loved science, excelled in English, and hated math. "Why should A be minus B?" she wondered. "Who the devil was X, anyway?" She won second place in a speech contest, wrote her first story, and earned a diploma in June 1918.

To those of us who live in an age where public school is free and available to all, it's easy to take Zora's educational accomplishments for granted. But in those years,

Zora said that while she was a student at Morgan Academy, she was put in charge of classes when teachers were absent. *Courtesy Beinecke Rare Book and Manuscript Library, Yale University*

a high-school education was generally unavailable to blacks, especially in the South. In 1916, the year before Zora entered Morgan, the black population in the United States numbered almost 11 million. Yet there were only sixty-seven black public high schools in the entire country, with fewer than twenty thousand students.

For Zora, a young black woman with no family support, no money, and no "resting place," earning a high-school diploma was a remarkable feat. That she went on to Howard University and then to Columbia University shows astonishing will power and intelligence. In "Walking on Fly-Paper," Zora explains how, despite the hardships of the Baltimore years, she resolved to pull out of the mud and do "something for my soul."

WALKING ON FLY-PAPER

Back, out walking on fly-paper again. Money was what I needed to get back in school. I could have saved a lot of money if I had received it. But the-atrical salaries being so uncertain, I did not get mine half the time. I had it when I had it, but when it was not paid I never worried. But now I needed it. Miss M—— was having her troubles, trying to help her folks she informed me by mail, so I never directly asked her for anything more. I had no resentment, either. It had all been very pleasant.

I tried waiting on table, and made a good wait-ress when my mind was on it, which was not often. I resented being patronized, more than the monot-ony of the job; those presumptuous cut-eye looks and supposed-to-be accidental touches on the thigh to see how I took to things. Men at the old game of "stealing a feel." People who paid for a quarter meal, left me a nickel tip, and then stood outside the door and nodded their heads for me to follow on and hear the rest of the story. But I was lacking in curiosity. I was not worrying so much about virtue. The thing just did not call me. There was neither the beauty of love, nor material advantage in it for me. After all, what is the use in having swine without pearls? Some educated men sat and talked about the things I was interested in, but if I seemed to listen, looked at me as much to say, "What would that mean to you?"

Then in the midst of other difficulties, I had to get sick. Not a sensible sickness for poor folks to have. No, I must get down with appendicitis and have to have an operation right away. So it was the free ward of the Maryland General Hospital for me.

When I was taken up to the amphitheatre for the operation I went up there placing a bet with God. I did not fear death. Nobody would miss me very much, and I had no treasures to leave behind me, so I would not go out of life looking backwards on that account. But I bet God that if I lived, I would try to find out the vague directions whispered in my ears and find the road it seemed that I must follow. How? When? Why? What? All those answers were hidden from me.

So two o'clock that day when they dressed me for surgery and took me up there in that room with the northern light and many windows, I stepped out of the chair before the nurse could interfere, walked to a window and took a good look out over Baltimore and the world as far as I could see, resigned myself to fate and, unaided, climbed upon the table, and breathed deeply when the ether cone was placed over my nose.

I scared the doctor and the nurses by not waking up until nine o'clock that night, but otherwise I was all right. I was alive, so I had to win my bet with God.

Soon, I had another waitress's job, trying to save money again, but I was only jumping up and down in my own foot-tracks.

I tried several other things but always I had that feeling that you have in a dream of trying to run, and sinking to your knees at every step in soft sticky mud. And this mud not only felt obscure to my feet, it smelled filthy to my nose. How to pull out?

How then did I get back to school? I just went. I got tired of trying to get the money to go. My clothes were practically gone. Nickeling and dimering along was not getting me anywhere. So I went to the night high school in Baltimore and that did something for my soul.

There I met the man who was to give me the key to certain things. In English, I was under Dwight O. W. Holmes. There is no more dynamic teacher anywhere under any skin. He radiates newness and nerve and says to your mind, "There is something wonderful to behold just ahead. Let's go see what it is." He is a pilgrim to the horizon. Anyway, that is the way he struck me. He made the way clear. Something about his face killed the drabness and discouragement in me. I felt that the thing could be done.

I turned in written work and answered questions like everybody else, but he took no notice of me particularly until one night in the study of English poets he read "Kubla Khan." You must get him to read it for you sometime. He is not a pretty man, but he has the face of a scholar, not dry and set like, but fire flashes from his deep-set eyes. His high-bridged, but sort of bent nose over his thin-lipped mouth . . . well, the whole thing reminds you of some old Roman like Cicero, Caesar or Virgil in tan skin.

That night, he liquefied the immortal brains of Coleridge, and let the fountain flow. I do not know whether something in my attitude attracted his attention, or whether what I had done previously made him direct the stream at me. Certainly every time he lifted his eyes from the page, he looked right into my eyes. It did not make me see him particularly, but it made me see the poem. That night seemed queer, but I am so visual-minded that all the other senses induce pictures in me. Listening to Coleridge's poem for the first time, I saw all that the writer had meant for me to see with him, and infinite cosmic things besides. I was not of the work-a-day world for days after Mr. Holmes's voice had ceased.

This was my world, I said to myself, and I shall be in it, and surrounded by it, if it is the last thing I do on God's green dirt-ball.

But he did something more positive than that. He stopped me after class and complimented me on my work. He did something else. He never asked me anything about myself, but he looked at me and toned his voice in such a way that I felt he knew all about me. His whole manner said, "No matter about the difficulties past and present, step on it!"

I went back to class only twice after that. I did not say a word to him about my resolve. But the next week, I went out to Morgan College to register in the high-school department.

After Morgan came Howard University in Washington, D.C., the school Zora called the "Negro Harvard." Helped again by friends (a teacher there remembered her as a "rough-edged diamond"), she took college preparatory courses in the school year 1918–19. She earned an associate degree in 1920 but could not afford the luxury of full-time studies to finish her degree. For six years, Zora was a part-time student, completing a year and a half of college work between 1919 and 1924.

The Howard years were busy ones. She attended class in the morning, worked from 3:30 P.M. until 8:30 P.M., then studied at night. Her job as a manicurist in a barber shop brought in twelve to fifteen dollars a week, including tips. The shop was near the White House, and Zora found herself "holding the hands" of senators and congressmen, who teased her, helped her with Greek lessons, and shared their intimate secrets. No doubt she repaid their confidences with her quick wit and funny tales. As one acquaintance remembered, Zora could get into a story "almost before you knew it."

In 1943, nineteen years after she left, Zora was given Howard University's Distinguished Alumni Award for her accomplishments. *Courtesy The Schomburg Center for Research in Black Culture, The New York Public Library, Astor Lenox and Tilden Foundations*

Her schedule didn't leave much time for social events, but she did become involved in Stylus, the campus literary club. Dr. Alain Locke headed this elite group of nineteen members. Locke had little use for women—on the first day of class he promised his female students an automatic C if they would not return. But even Locke, who expected and encouraged mediocrity in women, could not ignore Zora's gifts. Her English teachers urged her to enter the competition for membership. Zora was accepted, and she published her first short story in *Stylus* magazine in 1921.

She also wrote "Drenched in Light," the story of a joyous "little brown person" from Eatonville who sits on the gatepost and begs rides from travelers. In December 1924, "Drenched in Light" was published by a New York-based black magazine, *Opportunity: A Journal of Negro Life*. Charles S. Johnson, founder of *Opportunity*, used the magazine to introduce new black authors and their work to the public. He wrote to Zora and encouraged her to come to New York, where she could meet and work with equally talented writers.

After another illness, she had run out of money for tuition at Howard. In New York, she could satisfy her urge to write and try to finish her degree. Zora decided it was time to move on. Mama's child was on her way to making history as a member of the Harlem Renaissance.

◆ 4 ◆

HARLEM I

"And black men's feet learned roads. Some said good-bye cheerfully . . . others fearfully, with terrors of unknown dangers in their mouths . . . others in their eagerness for distance said nothing. The daybreak found them gone. The wind said North." This is Zora's description of the "Great Migration," when by 1920, three hundred thousand black workers had left the South and moved to northern cities.

North. The word that had symbolized freedom for blacks since the days of Harriet Tubman now meant freedom of a different sort. During 1915–16, the agricultural South had suffered economic blows from drought, floods, and the boll weevil. Wages were low. Compared to the rest of the country, southern black workers earned one-third less money for the same day's work. Housing, too, was substandard. Many blacks in the rural South lived in the same cabins that had housed slaves or in shacks built upon the foundation of earlier slave quarters.

With the vision of better wages and housing, thousands sought refuge from poverty, Jim Crowism, and lynchings. "Every time a lynching takes place in a community down South," one northern community official noted, "you can depend on it that colored people will arrive . . . in two weeks."

The North was no promised land—there were incidents of lynching, and segregation existed by custom, if not by law. Still, many blacks believed that their lot could only improve if they left the South.

Between 1910 and 1920, southern blacks poured into the section of Manhattan known as Harlem, doubling the population of New York City. As early as 1910, less than a quarter of Manhattan's blacks had been born in New York. Most were new arrivals from Georgia, the Carolinas, and Virginia.

The huge increase in population created a supportive climate for the arts. Harlem became a cultural magnet that attracted unknown musicians and artists. They were drawn to Harlem by awards and prizes being offered by white patrons and black magazines. Here they were free to develop their artistry and become part of the "golden legend" of Harlem.

Harlem also attracted poets and novelists who weren't satisfied with George Washington Carver's advice to blacks: Learn a trade and "lift your bucket where you are." Educated and talented, they came to Harlem to find success. In a ten-year burst of creativity, they wrote some of the most memorable literature of this century. Zora Neale Hurston was one of this small group of writers. Their literature reflects the spirit of Harlem in the twenties—a movement called the Harlem Renaissance.

On a May evening in 1925, Zora found herself in Manhattan, eating chicken and mashed potatoes with 316 people at the ritzy Fifth Avenue restaurant. The occasion was a gala awards dinner given by *Opportunity*. The magazine had sponsored a contest for black writers, and out of 732 entries, only 15 would receive awards. For months the excitement had been building. When the long banquet was over, Zora had won seventy dollars in cash prizes and four distinctions: two honorable mentions, second place for her play *Color Struck*, and second place for her short story "Spunk."

That night, Zora met many of the bright stars of the Harlem Renaissance, including Langston Hughes. Hughes would become the poet laureate of Harlem and was the only writer in the contest to win as many awards as Zora. "She's a clever girl, isn't she," Hughes remarked after meeting Zora. "I would like to know her." She also met people who could help her career: black critics, white publishers, and established authors.

The evening marked the official beginning of Zora's career. Her reputation had preceded her arrival in Harlem—she was already a published author in *Opportunity,* and Alain Locke, her professor from Howard, had pronounced her "the best and the brightest" of the promising writers. But the awards dinner gave her a new status. She was no longer an amateur writer. Now she was an artist, one of the New Negroes who would help create a "new soul" for the black race.

The invitation to *Opportunity*'s award dinner at which Zora's work was publicly recognized. The invitation was designed by Harlem Renaissance artist Winhold Reiss. *Courtesy Moorland-Spingarn Research Center, Howard University*

Her professional identity was further assured later that same year. When Locke edited *The New Negro,* an anthology of black writing that marked the literary beginning of the Harlem Renaissance, he included her award-winning story, "Spunk."

Like the other Harlem writers, Zora was long on talent, but short on money. When she came to Harlem, she had less than two dollars and no job. Within a few days, friends "had given her everything, from decorative silver birds . . . down to a footstool." Friends also found her a job as secretary to Fannie Hurst, a famous novelist who remembered that Zora had a "blazing zest for life."

By the fall of 1925, Zora had received a scholarship to Barnard College, the women's division of Columbia University. For the next two years, she studied anthropology and made her literary contributions to the Harlem Renaissance—poems, articles, plays, and short stories.

There are more stories *about* Zora than *by* her from those few years. From the moment she arrived, she made a vivid impression on everyone she met. Zora was boisterous—"I am running wild in every direction trying to see everything at once," she wrote to a friend. She was so unreliable that the secretary for *Opportunity* had to make sure Zora didn't miss interviews with Fannie Hurst and Barnard officials. "If something else interesting came up," recalled the secretary, "she was off."

Three stories have become part of the Zora legend. To disprove the popular notion that blacks' skulls were too small to hold normal-size brains, she stood on a

Zora during the New York years. She hosted a steady stream of
visitors: students, writers, musicians. *Courtesy Beinecke Rare
Book and Manuscript Library, Yale University*

street corner and measured the heads of complete strangers. And she once took a nickel from a blind man's cup, saying, "I need money worse than you today. Lend me this! Next time I'll give it back."

She also dared a friend to walk down the street with her while she smoked a Pall Mall cigarette. Smoking in public was a scandalous act for a woman in those days. Zora evidently enjoyed using the street as a theater for shocking behavior.

Outrageous as she was, Zora didn't drink. Harlem was famous for its cabarets and cocktail parties. "Life was a little wild at that time," according to one member of the Harlem Renaissance group. "Everybody drank too much." Zora was "an original," comfortable in her own skin without the help of alcohol.

In addition to *Opportunity*, Harlem was home to two other black magazines, the *Crisis* and the *Messenger*. The editors of all the magazines served as advisers to the up-and-coming writers. They provided encouragement, recognition, and even food and a bed when necessary. The magazines published the poetry and short stories of the group, including the works of Arna Bontemps, Jean Toomer, Claude McKay, Dorothy West, Countee Cullen, Nella Larsen, and Langston Hughes.

It was, for the most part, a male world. Of thirty-three writers whose works appeared in *The New Negro*, only six, including Zora, were women. Even among the few women of the Harlem Renaissance, Zora stood out.

Jessie Fauset, novelist and literary editor for the *Crisis*, was prim and ladylike, "gracious . . . with gentle eyes." Dorothy West, short-story author during the twenties, was petite. She recalls that she wasn't even considered competition by the men, who "were all very protective. . . . They went by my smallness."

In contrast, Zora was tall (five foot seven), a handsome woman who resembled her large, big-boned father. Her clothes matched her theatrical personality. Zora wore scarves, bangles, and beads, and she could usually be seen in some outlandish turban or fedora hat.

Different in looks and behavior, Zora also chose to live a life much different from that of most women of her time. Black women worked, but the only choice for many were agricultural or domestic jobs where they performed the same tasks that field and house slaves had a generation earlier.

For blacks who could attend college, "teaching and preaching" were the only jobs available. There were few female ministers, so teaching became the career route for women. In those years, educated black women started schools, colleges, and day-care centers, trying to close the literacy gap created by slavery: The year Zora was nineteen, three out of ten blacks could not sign their name.

Zora's decision to become an anthropologist and a writer made her rare indeed. Even the route she chose as a writer set her apart. The black women writers of her era combined a teaching career with journalism. They wrote society columns for newspapers or contributed to church magazines. Dorothy West remembers, "Women were always asked. 'What pseudonym do you use?' because a woman didn't write, didn't give her

Zora performing the Crow Dance, a game that originated in West Africa. *Courtesy Beinecke Rare Book and Manuscript Library, Yale University*

name . . . a [woman] writer meant someone who's got no respectable job."

So, there was Zora—a flamboyant woman who dared to be a writer. To top it off, she was from the South. The other Harlem writers were from every corner of the country—California, Washington State, New York, Philadelphia, Kansas. She alone was the southerner, to whom it was an everyday affair to hear somebody called a "mullet-headed, mule-eared, wall-eyed, hog-nosed, 'gator-faced, shad-mouthed, screw-necked, goat-bellied, puzzle-gutted, camel-backed, butt-sprung, battle-hammed, knock-kneed, razor-legged, box-ankled, shovel-footed, unmated [unmatched shoes] so-and-so!"

From Zora's southern background sprang her ability to create unforgettable folk characters and speech. It was a sign of her genius, but it would also be her downfall. W. E. B. Du Bois and other leaders of the Harlem Renaissance wanted writing "untainted by racial stereotype." To them, racial stereotype included folklore.

The portrayal of blacks as shiftless, happy-go-lucky banjo players would only pull the race down. If folklore was used, it had to be rewritten as literature for the sophisticated reader. It had to be artistic. Zora had been rocked in the cradle of Eatonville folkways, and her stories from the Harlem days reflected that culture. Her writing contained authentic folklore, but to many it was too primitive to be considered art.

This pattern of criticism that began in the Harlem years would haunt Zora's entire writing career. Reviewers complained that her writing had too much folklore and too little plot, that her characters were

Zora said of this picture, "I love myself . . . when I am looking
mean and impressive." Photograph by patron of the arts Carl
Van Vechten. *Courtesy the Estate of Carl Van Vechten. Joseph
Solomon, Executor. Beinecke Rare Book and Manuscript Library, Yale University*

drawn from only one part of the black population: ". . . the lowly, rural negro."

Other criticism would spring from reaction to her unique, sometimes annoying, personality. Zora did not fit the predictable role for a woman, even in the free-wheeling Roaring Twenties. She entertained, amused, and irritated, but she was not what men expected from a woman. Critics blinded by personal distaste for Zora the woman, could not fairly judge Zora the writer.

Twenty years after her death, black literary critics still commented more on Zora's unorthodox ways than on her writing. One critic called Zora quick-tempered and arrogant, declaring that her writing should be examined with this image in mind. Another attacked her "personal character" while calling her early writing "insignificant."

Until recently, Zora has received little positive recognition for her early Harlem stories. Now, after years of obscurity, her early writing is back in print and there is a new appreciation of her talent for weaving black folk culture into fiction.

"The Eatonville Anthology" is one of Zora's contributions to the Harlem Renaissance. A "grand storyteller," she was always the center of attention at parties. Zora kept her audience laughing by imitating Eatonville characters and retelling tales that she remembered from Joe Clarke's porch.

These short pieces are the written version of her party stories. They were originally published in 1926 by the *Messenger* and are a humorous combination of fact, fiction, and folklore.

· · · · ·

Zora in a photograph taken by Carl Van Vechten. She dedicated *Tell My Horse* to Van Vechten, calling him "God's image of a friend." *Courtesy the Estate of Carl Van Vechten. Joseph Solomon, Executor. Beinecke Rare Book and Manuscript Library, Yale University*

THE EATONVILLE ANTHOLOGY

II. TURPENTINE LOVE

JIM MERCHANT is always in good humor—even with his wife. He says he fell in love with her at first sight. That was some years ago. She has had all her teeth pulled out, but they still get along splendidly.

He says the first time he called on her he found out that she was subject to fits. This didn't cool his love, however. She had several in his presence.

One Sunday, while he was there, she had one, and her mother tried to give her a dose of turpentine to stop it. Accidentally, she spilled it in her eye and it cured her. She never had another fit, so they got married and have kept each other in good humor ever since.

III.

BECKY MOORE has eleven children of assorted colors and sizes. She has never been married, but that is not her fault. She has never stopped any of the fathers of her children from proposing, so if she has no father for her children it's not her fault. The men round about are entirely to blame.

The other mothers of the town are afraid that it is catching. They won't let their children play with hers.

VII. VILLAGE FICTION

JOE LINDSAY is said by Lum Boger to be the largest manufacturer of prevarications in Eatonville;

Brazzle (late owner of the world's leanest and meanest mule) contends that his business is the largest in the state and his wife holds that he is the biggest liar in the world.

Exhibit A—He claims that while he was in Orlando one day he saw a doctor cut open a woman, remove everything—liver, lights and heart included—clean each of them separately; the doctor then washed out the empty woman, dried her out neatly with a towel and replaced the organs so expertly that she was up and about her work in a couple of weeks.

VIII.

SEWELL is a man who lives all to himself. He moves a great deal. So often, that 'Lige Moseley says his chickens are so used to moving that every time he comes out into his backyard the chickens lie down and cross their legs, ready to be tied up again.

He is baldheaded; but he says he doesn't mind that, because he wants as little as possible between him and God.

IX.

MRS. CLARKE is Joe Clarke's wife. She is a soft-looking, middle-aged woman, whose bust and stomach are always holding a get-together.

She waits on the store sometimes and cries every time he yells at her which he does every time she makes a mistake, which is quite often. She calls her husband "Jody." They say he used to beat her in the store when he was a young man, but he is not so impatient now. He can wait until he goes home.

She shouts in Church every Sunday and shakes the hand of fellowship with everybody in the Church with her eyes closed, but somehow always misses her husband.

XIV.

ONCE 'WAY BACK YONDER before the stars fell all the animals used to talk just like people. In them days dogs and rabbits was the best of friends—even tho both of them was stuck on the same gal—which was Miss Nancy Coon. She had the sweetest smile and the prettiest striped and bushy tail to be found anywhere.

They both run their legs nigh off trying to win her for themselves—fetching nice ripe persimmons and such. But she never give one or the other no satisfaction.

Finally one night Mr. Dog popped the question right out. "Miss Coon," he says, "Ma'am, also Ma'am, which would you ruther be—a lark flyin' or a dove a settin'?"

'Course Miss Nancy she blushed and laughed a little and hid her face behind her bushy tail for a spell. Then she said sorter shy like, "I does love yo' sweet voice, brother dawg—but—I ain't jes' exactly set my mind yit."

Her and Mr. Dog set on a spell, when up comes hopping Mr. Rabbit wid his tail fresh washed and his whiskers shining. He got right down to business and asked Miss Coon to marry him, too.

"Oh, Miss Nancy," he says, "Ma'am, also Ma'am, if you'd see me settin' straddle of a mud-cat leadin' a minnow, what would you think? Ma'am also Ma'am?" Which is a out and out proposal as everybody knows.

"Youse awful nice, Brother Rabbit, and a beautiful dancer, but you cannot sing like Brother Dog. Both you uns come back next week to gimme time for to decide."

They both left arm-in-arm. Finally Mr. Rabbit says to Mr. Dog, "T'ain't no use in me going back—she ain't gwinter have me. So I mought as well give up. She loves singing, and I ain't got nothing but a squeak."

"Oh, don't talk that a way," says Mr. Dog, tho' he is glad Mr. Rabbit can't sing none.

"Thass all right, Brer Dog. But if I had a sweet voice like you got, I'd have it worked on and make it sweeter."

"How! How! How!" Mr. Dog cried, jumping up and down.

"Lemme fix it for you, like I do for Sister Lark and Sister Mockingbird."

"When? Where?" asked Mr. Dog, all excited. He was figuring that if he could sing just a little better Miss Coon would be bound to have him.

"Just you meet me t'morrer in de huckleberry patch," says the rabbit and off they both goes to bed.

The dog is there on time next day and after a while the rabbit comes loping up.

"Mawnin', Brer Dawg," he says kinder chippy like. "Ready to git yo' voice sweetened?"

"Sholy, sholy, Brer Rabbit. Let's we all hurry about it. I wants tuh serenade Miss Nancy from the piney woods tuh night."

"Well, den, open yo' mouf and poke out yo' tongue," says the rabbit.

No sooner did Mr. Dog poke out his tongue than Mr. Rabbit split it with a knife and ran for all he was worth to a hollow stump and hid hisself.

The dog has been mad at the rabbit ever since.

Anybody who don't believe it happened, just look at the dog's tongue and he can see for himself where the rabbit slit it right up the middle.

Stepped on a tin, mah story ends.

◆ 5 ◆
HARLEM II

Zora was the most amusing member of the Harlem group, but she also had a stubborn, even unpleasant, streak. One incident toward the end of her Harlem years shows this side of her personality. The conflict centered around Mrs. Charlotte Mason, a wealthy white patron who used her money to finance and control the creative output of Zora, Langston Hughes, and other Harlem Renaissance writers, painters, and sculptors.

Mrs. Mason gave over fifty thousand dollars to the struggling artists, who needed the money to survive and develop their talents. She insisted that they call her "Godmother," encouraging an emotional dependency as well as a financial one. Sitting in a large chair with her subjects at her feet, she presided over her Park Avenue penthouse like a queen. To Langston, the "busboy poet," and Zora, who knew the smell of poverty,

Charlotte Mason, Zora's patron. She called Mrs. Mason "the world's most gallant woman," but she noted that Mrs. Mason's tongue was sharp, "bleeding your vanity like a rusty nail." *Courtesy Beinecke Rare Book and Manuscript Library, Yale University*

the sight of Mrs. Mason's "caviar and gleaming silver" must have made her seem like a fairy godmother.

But strings were attached to the gifts. Langston received one hundred fifty dollars a month from Mrs. Mason while he wrote his first novel. She demanded a detailed account of his expenses ("taxi-fare, postage stamps, Bromo-Seltzer") and revised his book as he wrote it. ". . . it is apparent," she arrogantly said to him, "that you had no training in literary expression as a little child, and in college."

Over a five-year period beginning in 1927, Mrs. Mason gave Zora fifteen thousand dollars to finance folklore-collecting trips. The money was carefully doled out at two hundred dollars a month, and Zora had to give a strict account of how each dollar was spent, down to money for medicine and a pair of shoes. "I really need a pair of shoes," she wrote her employer. "My big toe is about to burst out of my right shoe and so I must do something about it."

As Zora wrote down the tales that would eventually become *Mules and Men*, she sent them back to New York, where they were held in Mrs. Mason's safe-deposit box. Godmother controlled the material, including the power to censor "the dirty words" she found in the folktales Zora had collected.

Zora aptly described their relationship as curious. She was convinced that Mrs. Mason used telepathic powers to communicate with her godchildren, sending them messages from across the country. Furthermore, Zora believed she was the only one who could read Godmother's mind in return. She felt a bond with the older woman, but it is hard to say where this sense of

Langston Hughes as a young writer. *Courtesy Moorland-Spingarn Research Center, Howard University*

kinship ended and financial need began. If Zora admired Mrs. Mason, she also depended on her for the clothes on her back.

Zora paid a stiff price for Mrs. Mason's patronage. In exchange for the money, she signed a contract to publish her collected folklore only in a form approved by her patron. This did not include plays or novels. Mrs. Mason thought these money-making ventures would ruin the primitive soul of the "raucous sayings and doings of the Negro farthest down."

Despite Mrs. Mason's objections to dramatizing folklore, Zora was eager to present it on the stage. During the late twenties, she and Langston planned a folk play, sharing ideas when both were in New York, exchanging letters when one was away.

In 1930, they collaborated on a play called *Mule Bone*, a three-act comedy based on a folktale collected by Zora. She was to provide the style for the play—the jokes and folk sayings—and he was to create the plot. Both were broke as usual, and Langston suggested that they pay their typist by making her a third collaborator and business manager of the play's production. Zora was unwilling to share writing credit or possible royalties with a third party whom she didn't like, anyway. Without telling Langston, she sent the play off for copyright with only her name on it.

Langston threatened to sue, and Zora stubbornly wrote to him, "It was my story from beginning to end. It is my dialogue; my situation." During an argument over production of the play, Langston claimed that she "made such a scene as you can not possibly imagine. She pushed her hat back, bucked her eyes, ground her teeth, and shook manuscripts in my face. . . ." He wondered to a friend if she was crazy.

With some prodding from Zora, Mrs. Mason refused to hear Langston's version and sided with Zora in the dispute. Langston lost his wealthy patron's financial and emotional support. Devastated, he ended his relationship with both women.

The play, a brave attempt to present authentic black folklore, was never staged or even printed in its entirety. Sadly, Zora and Langston, who had advised and encouraged one another for years, each lost a friend. Hughes retaliated years later in his autobiography by calling Zora the "perfect darkie" for her white friends. Zora barely mentioned him in her autobiography. The break was final, and to some it marked the end of the Harlem Renaissance.

Zora's fellow writers, including Langston Hughes and more recent black literary critics, cited the *Mule Bone* affair as proof that she would do anything to get ahead. They felt Zora was an "Aunt Jemima" hypocrite who took money from a white patron (though many others did), that she tried to steal credit for Langston's work, and that she used "extravagant flattery" to get attention from those who could help her career. "Zora Neale Hurston," one writer says, "would have conned her way to China to find recognition."

Although the *Mule Bone* incident was unfortunate, it is only fair to remember that Langston Hughes could be as shrewd as Zora in seeking success. He, too, accepted money from Mrs. Mason. Langston also used flattery on those who could publish his writing. Both

Langston and Zora were cunning. He was simply quieter about it.

Zora wrote eight plays in all. Her dream was to see black folk material presented on stage "unhampered . . . so that people may see what we are really like." In *Mule Bone*, she and Langston Hughes created characters who spoke in the colorful style that was typical of black folklore. They hoped to show that black speech was an art in itself.

The following courting ritual from *Mule Bone* is a verbal contest similar to the lying sessions on Joe Clarke's porch. The man who can best "talk for" his woman will win her with his skillful use of words.

The play is set in Eatonville. The three characters are walking down a railroad track in a Florida forest. Earlier, Jim has fought with Dave over Daisy and hit him in the head with a mule bone. In this last scene, they compete for Daisy in a less violent way—a ritual designed to win her affection with wild claims and witty rhymes.

COURTING RITUAL

DAVE TO DAISY:
I love you harder than de thunder can bump a stump—if I don't—God's a gopher.

JIM TO DAISY:
You ain't never give me no chance to talk wid you right.

DAISY TO BOTH:
Aw, you'all better stop dat. You know you don't mean it.

DAVE TO DAISY:
Who don't mean it. Lemme you tell you somethin, mama, if you was mine, I wouldn't have you countin no [railroad] ties wid you pretty lil toes. Know whut I'd do. . . . I'd buy a whole passenger train and hire some mens to run it for you.

JIM TO DAISY:
De wind may blow, de door may slam, Dat stuff you shooting ain't worth a dam. I'd buy you a great big ole ship—and then, baby, I'd buy you a ocean to sail yo ship on.

DAVE TO JIM:
A long train, a short caboose, Dat lie whut you shootin, ain't no use. . . . Miss Daisy, know what I'd do for you? I'd come down de river ridin a mud cat [a large fish] and leadin a minnow.

JIM TO DAISY:
Naw he ain't—he's just lyin—he's a noble liar. Know whut I'd do if you was mine? . . . I'd make a panther wash you dishes and a gator chop yo wood for you.

DAVE TO JIM:
How much time would you do for Daisy on the chain gang?

JIM TO DAVE:
Twenty years and like it.

DAVE TO DAISY:

See dat, Daisy, Dat nigger ain't willin to do no time for you. I'd beg de judge to gimme life. [Both Jim and Dave laugh.] Don't you be skeered, baby. Papa kin take keer o you.

DAVE TO JIM:

[Counting his fingers] Countin from de finger back to de thumb? . . . Start anything, I got you some.

JIM TO DAVE:

Aw, I don't want no more fight wid you, Dave.

DAVE TO JIM:

Who said anything about fighting? We just provin who love Daisy de best.

◆ 6 ◆
FLORIDA

In folklore as in all other forms of human behavior, the world is a great big old serving platter and all the localities are like eating-plates. All of the plates get helped with food from the platter, but each plate seasons to suit itself . . . that is what is known as originality.

Zora Neale Hurston

Zora Hurston's career as a folklorist began in 1927 with two trips to Florida. Zora knew that folklore, like the people who pass it on, can grow, change, move, and die. She wanted to record the old-time tales from the Eatonville plate and "set them down before it's too late."

Southern black folklore had never been collected by one of the "folk." Zora was especially qualified for the task because she had grown up in the very culture she wanted to save. Who but Zora could recapture the "lyin" sessions of her childhood? Besides, to hear the

stories and songs of her youth would be like finding
some of the lost, happier years before her mother's
death.

Columbia University sponsored the trip, and financial support came from Carter Woodson, an important
black historian of the twenties. Woodson was founder of
the Association for the Study of Negro Life and History

Zora with "Sassy Susie" in the background. *Courtesy Beinecke
Rare Book and Manuscript Library, Yale University*

and creator of Negro History Week. He provided a fourteen hundred dollar fellowship to pay Zora's expenses. Such impressive backing testifies to her reputation at Columbia as a talented scholar.

But despite the support, Zora's trip was unsuccessful. As she later said, collecting folklore is not as easy as it sounds. She had left her hometown years before as a child and returned as an educated woman who had been "up North." The old stories just didn't flow for a woman in a fancy dress who drove her own car (nicknamed "Sassy Susie" by Zora). She later recalled that she didn't gather enough folklore to make a flea a waltzing jacket.

It was during this trip that Zora secretly married Herbert Sheen, a fellow student she had met her first year in college. "For the first time since my mother's death," she wrote in her autobiography, "there was someone who felt really warm and close to me."

There were immediate problems. Sheen wanted to go to medical school in Chicago, but Zora was almost through with her college studies. Now a trained anthropologist, she was unwilling to follow her husband, and neither Sheen nor Zora could give up promising careers. The marriage lasted only eight months. Letters from Zora to Sheen show that they remained friends for the rest of her life. In 1953, she wrote to him, "Your own mother has never loved you to the depth I have, Herbert. . . ."

After six months of fruitless collecting in Eatonville, Zora returned to New York and cried "salty tears" of disappointment over her failure to gather folklore. It was then that she met Mrs. Mason. She signed the con-

After Zora returned to New York from her folklore-collecting trip to Florida, she completed course work at Barnard and received her degree in 1928. *Courtesy Beinecke Rare Book and Manuscript Library, Yale University*

tract to collect folklore for Mason, and made plans for a second trip to Florida.

Anxious to try again, she "kicked the little Chevrolet right along" and hurried back to Eatonville. This time the trip was a success. Zora had learned a lesson about the collecting process. "I had to go back, dress as they did, talk as they did, live their life," she recalled, "so I could get into my stories the world I knew as a child."

Zora moved in with a childhood friend and invited the more talkative citizens of Eatonville over for gingerbread and buttermilk. They repaid her with enough "lies" to fill a book. Before starting a tale, each story teller recited a rhyme to get his "wind on."

> De rooster chew t'backer, de hen dip snuff
> De biddy can't do it, but he struts his stuff.

> or

> Once upon a time was a good old time
> Monkey chew tobacco and spit white lime.

Then they took turns telling John and Massa lies, Jack tales, and creation stories: The day God gave out color, the folks crowded around to listen. "Git back! Git back!" God said, but they thought he said, "Git black!"

Zora was invited to a toe party, a hilarious social event where the ladies stood behind a sheet and stuck out their toes. After looking over the display, the gentlemen bought a toe for a dime. The owner of the toe was then treated to refreshments and dancing. Zora's toe was sold five times, but after five helpings of chicken, she recalled, she had to "get another stomach or quit eating."

That night Babe Brown picked his "box" (guitar) and Johnnie Barton played piano. Zora heard a folk song about the infamous Polk County:

> Polk County! Ah!
> Where the water tastes like cherry wine

Polk County was a rough-and-tumble mix of sawmills, phosphate mines, and turpentine camps. It was also home to the best liars in Florida. Eager to hear the "poets of the swinging blade," Zora said good-bye to her hometown and headed the Chevy to the jook joints of Polk County.

The folks in Polk County worked hard by day and played hard by night. To forget the screaming saw of the mill and the sweat of the mine, they flocked after dark to jooks, where "pay night rocks on with music and gambling and laughter and dancing and fights." Even confident Zora felt as "timid as an egg without a shell" in Polk County—she knew that she would need protection in this rowdy environment.

She made friends with Big Sweet, a large, knife-toting woman whose authority was unquestioned by both black workers and white bosses. Big Sweet directed Zora to good storytellers and judged her lying contests. She also made it clear that anyone messing with Zora would have to tangle with Big Sweet first.

One evening, Zora made the mistake of going to a jook joint alone. She intended to collect some stories by joining the men in a woofing (casual talking) session. But a jealous woman named Lucy didn't care for the way Zora sweet-talked the men. She blocked the only door to the jook and drew a knife on Zora. Big Sweet

Zora Neale Hurston collecting folklore in Eatonville, 1935. Zora accompanied two other folklorists on a collecting trip for the Library of Congress. As the only black in the group, she was crucial to the success of the expedition. One of her colleagues, Alan Lomax, wrote that Zora was "probably the best-informed person today on Western Negro folklore." *Courtesy Library of Congress*

appeared and held Lucy off with a kick to the knees. As double-edged razors flew and blood ran, Zora sneaked out the door, threw her car into high gear "just too quick," and made her escape.

Daytime was a little safer for collecting tales, so Zora joined Big Sweet and some sawmill workers on a fishing trip. A day off was rare, and spirits ran high as they gathered their bait and homemade trout lines. The group walked through moss-hung trees, swinging their poles and woofing the entire two miles to the lake. Zora heard how the 'gator lost his tongue, why the possum has no hair on his tail, and why the mockingbird won't fly on Friday. Each member tried to top the other's tall tale. And when the talk turned to mosquitoes, the lying got serious.

"Mosquito Lies" is taken from *Mules and Men*, the first book to record black folklore exactly as the people said it. Published in 1935, *Mules and Men* demonstrates Zora Hurston's unique methods of collecting folklore. She described her own collecting experiences, such as pretending to be a bootlegger to explain her new car. She also included the names of her contributors, an uncommon practice in retelling folklore. Zora's methods allow the reader to meet the storytellers—to experience black rural Florida as it was sixty years ago through the lies of Will, Joe, Sack Daddy, and Black Baby.

MOSQUITO LIES

Will House said, "Ah know a lie on a black gnat. Me and my buddy Joe Wiley was ramshackin' Georgy over when we come to a loggin' camp. So bein' out of work we ast for a job. So de man puts us on and gives us some oxes to drive. Ah had a six-yoke team and Joe was drivin' a twelve-yoke team. As we was comin' thru de woods we heard somethin' hummin' and we didn't know what it was. So we got hungry and went in a place to eat and when we come out a gnat had done et up de six-yoke team and de twelve-yoke team, and was sittin' up on de wagon pickin' his teeth wid a ox-horn and cryin' for somethin' to eat."

"Yeah," put in Joe Wiley, "we seen a man tie his cow and calf out to pasture and a mosquito come along and et up de cow and was ringin' de bell for de calf."

"Dat wasn't no full-grown mosquito at dat," said Eugene Oliver. "Ah was travellin' in Texas and laid down and went to sleep. De skeeters bit me so hard till Ah seen a ole iron wash-pot, so Ah crawled under it and turned it down over me good so de skeeters couldn't git to me. But you know dem skeeters bored right thru dat iron pot. So I up wid a hatchet and bradded their bills into de pot. So they flew on off 'cross Galveston Bay wid de wash-pot on their bills."

"Look," said Black Baby, "on de Indian River we went to bed and heard de mosquitoes singin' like bull alligators. So we got under four blankets. Shucks! Dat wasn't nothin'. Dem mosquitoes just screwed off dem short bills, reached back in they hip-pocket and took out they long bills and screwed 'em on and come right on through dem blankets and got us."

"Is dat de biggest mosquito you all ever seen? Shucks! Dey was li'l baby mosquitoes! One day my ole man took some men and went out into de woods to cut some fence posts. And a big rain come up so they went up under a great big ole tree. It was so big it would take six men to meet around it. De other men set down on de roots but my ole man stood up and leaned against de tree. Well, sir, a big old skeeter come up on de other side of dat tree and bored right thru it and got blood out of my ole man's back. Dat made him so mad till he up wid his ax and bradded dat mosquito's bill into dat tree. By dat time de rain stopped and they all went home.

"Next day when they come out, dat mosquito had done cleaned up ten acres dying. And two or three weeks after dat my ole man got enough bones from dat skeeter to fence in dat ten acres."

Everybody liked to hear about the mosquito. They laughed all over themselves.

"Yeah," said Sack Daddy, "you sho is tellin' de truth 'bout dat big ole mosquito 'cause my ole man bought dat same piece of land and raised a crop of pumpkins on it and lemme tell y'all right now— mosquito dust is de finest fertilizer in de world. Dat land was so rich and we raised pumpkins so big dat we et five miles up in one of 'em and five miles down and ten miles acrost one and we ain't never found out how far it went. But my ole man was buildin' a scaffold inside so we could cut de pumpkin meat without so much trouble, when he dropped his hammer. He tole me, he says, 'Son, Ah done dropped my hammer. Go git it for me.' Well, Ah went down in de pumpkin and began to hunt dat hammer. Ah was foolin' 'round in there all day, when I met a man and he ast me what Ah was lookin' for. Ah tole him my ole man had done dropped his hammer and sent me to find it for

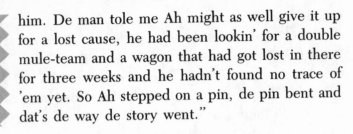

him. De man tole me Ah might as well give it up for a lost cause, he had been lookin' for a double mule-team and a wagon that had got lost in there for three weeks and he hadn't found no trace of 'em yet. So Ah stepped on a pin, de pin bent and dat's de way de story went."

◆ 7 ◆

NEW ORLEANS

In the heat of August 1928, Zora decided to "head my toenails" to Louisiana. She drove Sassy Susie from Polk County to New Orleans, the voodoo capital of America, where she hoped to study voodoo routines with the top conjure doctors. Zora was afraid that this type of folklore would soon be forgotten, for voodoo's greatest era was "forty years in the past." The second half of her folklore book, *Mules and Men*, relates what she learned about voodoo, or hoodoo, as it is called in America.

Voodoo's roots are in Africa. The captured slaves who were brought to the Americas represented a variety of African tribes. Each tribe had its own gods and methods of worship. Once in the New World, the slaves combined these various elements, and a new folk religion was created. Many of the slaveholders in Louisiana were Catholic, so as slaves absorbed the Christian customs of their owners, more ingredients were added to the religion.

71

Voodoo is still prevalent in parts of Africa, the southern states, and the Caribbean Islands. Knowledge of voodoo is secretly passed among believers by word of mouth and its practice is so secretive that no one is certain how many believers exist. Sixty years ago, Zora estimated them to be in the thousands. Now there are more than four million in Haiti alone.

Voodoo is based on a belief in magic and supernatural forces. It involves chants, prayers, songs, dances, and the ritual sacrifice of animals—commonly sheep, goats, and chickens. The rituals are presided over by conjure, or "two-headed," [twice as smart] doctors. These priests are consulted for matters pertaining to every aspect of life. They are called upon to cure illness, bury the dead, change the direction of a romance, and even bring harm or death to an enemy.

Talismans play an important role in voodoo ceremonies. "Anything may be conjure," Zora observed, "and nothing may be conjure." A shell wrapped in human hair might be used to bring love, a voodoo doll to signify death. Some talismans, such as candles, pictures of saints, and the Bible, show the influence of Catholicism on voodoo.

Zora was eager to collect voodoo folklore before "the white folks" could "grab our stuff and ruin it." But she was not just a scientist eager to investigate what most people considered superstitious orgies. She recognized that voodoo was a system of faith no stranger than any other religion. She compared the voodoo worship of water to baptism, and animal sacrifice to communion. "Any religion that satisfies the individual urge," she believed, "is valid for that person."

Zora had a great respect for black culture and a sincere desire to learn. But voodoo was against the law in New Orleans, and she had to convince the conjure doctors that her intentions were genuine. After a lot of waiting and "stumbling and asking," she gained their trust. They allowed her to visit secret rooms off back alleys, to see hidden voodoo altars, and to witness animal sacrifice in the moonlit dampness of the swamps.

Zora studied with six doctors. Most of them required an initiation rite that would qualify her as a pupil. From one doctor, she earned the Crown of Power (a coil of snakeskins) by fasting and lying naked on a couch in front of an altar for sixty-nine hours. In another ceremony, Zora became a doctor's apprentice. As two long pink candles burned, she was bathed in a warm bath of salt, sugar, perfume, and a pint of "strong parsley water." Then she was given a Bible to read and told what spirits to ask for a particular favor.

In a complicated rite called the Pea Vine Candle Drill, she lit eight blue candles with one black one. The candles were set in front of the altar in the curling shape of a serpent. Zora was led, then carried, through the maze of candles. With this rite, she became the Boss of Candles, or one who works with spirits.

For five months, Zora was a student of voodoo rites. She was one of the first to observe such ceremonies. Did Zora Hurston actually believe in voodoo powers? She found the rituals both "beautiful and terrifying," but Zora was obviously baffled when she says in this chilling excerpt from *Mules and Men*, "I don't know . . . always I have to say the same thing. I don't know. I don't know."

THE BLACK CAT BONE

When several of my jobs had turned out satisfactorily to Father Watson, he said to me, "You will do well, but you need the Black Cat Bone. Sometimes you have to be able to walk invisible. Some things must be done in deep secret, so you have to walk out of the sight of man."

First I had to get ready even to try this most terrible of experiences—getting the Black Cat Bone.

First we had to wait on the weather. When a big rain started, a new receptacle was set out in the yard. It could not be put out until the rain actually started for fear the sun might shine in it. The water must be brought inside before the weather faired off for the same reason. If lightning shone on it, it was ruined.

We finally got the water for the bath and I had to fast and "seek," shut in a room that had been purged by smoke. Twenty-four hours without food except a special wine that was fed to me every four hours. It did not make me drunk in the accepted sense of the word. I merely seemed to lose my body, my mind seemed very clear.

When dark came, we went out to catch a black cat. I must catch him with my own hands. Finding and catching black cats is hard work, unless one has been released for you to find. Then we repaired to a prepared place in the woods and a circle drawn and "protected" with nine horseshoes. Then the fire and the pot were made ready. A roomy iron pot with a lid. When the water boiled I was to toss in the terrified, trembling cat.

When he screamed, I was told to curse him. He screamed three times, the last time weak and resigned. The lid was clamped down, the fire kept vigorously alive. At midnight the lid was lifted. Here was the moment! The bones of the cat must be passed through my mouth until one tasted bitter.

Suddenly, the Rooster and Mary rushed in close to the pot and he cried, "Look out! This is liable to kill you. Hold your nerve!" They both looked fearfully around the circle. They communicated some unearthly terror to me. Maybe I went off in a trance. Great beast-like creatures thundered up to the circle from all sides. Indescribable noises, sights, feelings. Death was at hand! Seemed unavoidable! I don't know. Many times I have thought and felt, but I always have to say the same thing. I don't know. I don't know.

Before day I was home, with a small white bone for me to carry.

◆ 8 ◆

JAMAICA

Zora's fascination with voodoo continued into the thirties. She was especially interested in the use of plants as medicine and poison. "The greatest power of voodoo," she believed, "rests upon poisons and their antidotes."

In 1936, Zora decided to explore the folklore of the Caribbean Islands. A Guggenheim Fellowship financed her two-year trip to Jamaica and Haiti. The folklore she gathered on the two islands became her book *Tell My Horse*.

Zora knew that both these islands were the perfect place to study the relationship between Africa and black folklore, since the black population in the Caribbean is descended from slaves. Jamaica, in particular, could provide proof of the African connection. It is a lush, green island with an abundance of vegetation. Jamaican slaves might easily have adapted their African poison recipes by using the plants available in Jamaica.

Zora spent six months with the Maroons—an isolated group of people living high in the west Jamaican mountains. The Maroons are descended from fugitive slaves who fled to the mountains in 1655. When Zora visited them, they were living much as they had three centuries before. They built thatched huts, wore masks and costumes, and performed African songs and dances.

To get to the Maroon settlement, Zora rode a train high up in the hills to the end of the line. A "wall-eyed, pot-bellied" mule was sent to help her climb the last mountain peak. Zora thought she and the mule might be "sisters under the skin," but the mule disagreed. She took one look at Zora's gaudy orange necktie and threw her off within a half mile. Zora climbed the rest of the mountain on foot. At least the pop-eyed mule was honest, Zora remembered: "She never pretended to like me."

With typical Zora enthusiasm, she was eager to share the lives of the people she studied. When she saw that there was not one cooking stove in the village, she designed and helped build one of sheet tin, stovepipe, and cement. This was a great luxury for the women, who had to squat by open fires to prepare a meal. "We were really joyful," she said, "when we fired it the next day and found out that it worked."

Zora had learned from her experiences in Florida and New Orleans that patient waiting was the key to collecting folklore. Only by settling in to watch and observe could she see the Maroon culture in its natural form. She knew that if she asked to see a ceremony, she would see only a staged performance, not the real thing. And if she wanted to learn about poisons and antidotes, she must first establish a friendship with Medicine Man.

"So I just sat around and waited," Zora wrote in *Tell My Horse*. ". . . he took to coming around to talk with me." Medicine Man warmed to Zora, and one evening as they talked he performed an amazing demonstration for her. Millions of tree frogs were singing on the mountain peak across the valley. Medicine Man stood up, and with one quick motion, he ordered the frogs to stop. There was a deafening silence. Then, with a wave of his hand, "like an orchestra under the conductor's baton," he commanded them to sing. Astounded, Zora heard the "frog symphony" begin again.

Eventually, Medicine Man trusted Zora enough to show her his arts. In "Horse Bath and Bitters," she describes her visits with the Maroon doctor and the primitive medicines, poisons, and antidotes that he used.

HORSE BATH AND BITTERS

First we talked about things that are generally talked about in Jamaica. Brother Anansi, the Spider, that great culture hero of West Africa who is personated in Haiti by Ti Malice and in the United States by Brer Rabbit. About duppies and how and where they existed, and how to detect them. I learned that they lived mostly in silk-cotton trees and in almond trees. One should never plant either of those trees too close to the house because the duppies will live in them and "throw heat" on the people as they come and go about the house. One can tell when a duppy is near by the feeling of heat and the swelling of the head. A duppy can swell one's head to a huge thing just by being near. But if one drinks tea from that branch of the snake weed family known as Spirit Weed, duppies can't touch you. You can walk into a room where all kinds of evil and duppies are and be perfectly safe.

After a night or two of talk, the medicine man began to talk about his profession and soon I was a spectator while he practised his arts. I learned of the terrors and benefits of Cow-itch and of that potent plant known as Madame Fate. "It is a cruel weed." He told me, and I found he had understated its powers. I saw him working with the Cassada bean, the Sleep-and-Wake, Horse Bath and Marjo Bitters. Boil five leaves of Horse Bath and drink it with a pinch of salt and your kidneys are cleaned out magnificently. Boil six leaves and drink it and you will die. Marjo Bitter is a vine that grows on rocks. Take a length from your elbow to your wrist and make a tea and it is a most excellent medicine. Boil a length to the palm of your hand and you are violently poisoned. He used the bark of a tree called Jessamy, well boiled for a purgative. Twelve minutes after drinking the wine glass of medicine the purge begins and keeps up for five days without weakening the patient or griping.

I went with him to visit the "God wood" tree (Birch Gum). It is called "God wood" because it is the first tree that ever was made. It is the original tree of good and evil. He had a covenant with that tree on the sunny side. We went there more than once. One day we went there to prevent the enemies of the medicine man from harming him. He took a strong nail and a hammer with him and drove the nail into the tree up to the head with three strokes; dropped the hammer and walked away rapidly without looking back. Later on, he sent me back to fetch the hammer to him.

He proved to me that all you need to do to poison a person and leave them horribly swollen was to touch a chip of this tree to their skin while they were sweating. It was uncanny.

◆ 9 ◆
HAITI

Haiti lies one hundred miles to the east of Jamaica. Three centuries after the Spanish and the French brought 900,000 slaves to work the Haitian sugar plantations, remnants of West African culture remain intact. For Zora, Haiti was a rich mine of folklore, and she made two trips there between 1937 and 1938 to explore voodoo. After New Orleans and Jamaica, Zora was no stranger to voodoo, but Haiti's intricate rites eventually frightened her into leaving the island.

Her stay was intense. She photographed a zombie, wrote a novel in seven weeks, experienced a near-fatal illness, and gathered enough information to finish *Tell My Horse*.

The title for *Tell My Horse* comes from the powerful god of black humor, Guedé. The god of sarcasm and ridicule, Guedé drinks raw rum mixed with hot pepper. He shows himself by invisibly "mounting" a person's back. Guedé then speaks through the possessed "mount" and uses him to insult others. Zora noted that Haitians used the phrase "Tell my horse" as a cover—those who wanted to taunt someone would pretend to be Guedé's "mount."

She witnessed a test to tell if Guedé was present: A "true" mount who washed his face with Guedé's favorite drink was protected from the sting of rum and pepper in his eyes. "Those really 'mounted' do it without being told," Zora claimed, "and it never seems to injure them." Those who refused the test were fake mounts who used Guedé as an excuse to be rude.

When Zora untangled the complexities of voodoo gods in Haiti, she discovered that they were divided into two groups: the Rada gods, headed by Damballah, "the father of all that is powerful and good," and the Petro gods, who are evil.

She had been warned by Haitian friends not to study the evil Petro gods, but she was too curious to miss a Petro ceremony called "taking the spirit from the head of the dead." During the ritual, an evil spirit possessed a man in the crowd. Terrified, Zora watched his face disintegrate into a "horrible mask." After much praying by the voodoo priest, the good spirits or loa, banished the evil spirit. "The man fell," Zora wrote. "His body relaxed and his features untangled themselves and became a face again."

Zora, sensing an "unspeakable evil," was deeply frightened by the experience. Her voodoo studies had allowed her to witness things rarely seen by the outside world, but now she felt a sense of danger. And the more she studied voodoo poisons, the more her uneasiness increased.

She discovered one recipe for poison that used hair from a horse's tail. "Chop it up short and mix it in something like mush and give it to the one you wish to kill," Zora wrote. "The short bits of hair will penetrate the tissues like so many needles and each bit will then irritate, then puncture the intestines . . . the intestines will become full of sores and death is certain."

When Zora became violently ill in Haiti, she may have been convinced that she was, in fact, poisoned—a warning to stop any further voodoo studies. "I HAVE HAD A VIOLENT GASTRIC DISTURBANCE," she wrote to a friend. "For a whole day and night I'd thought I'd never make it." Frightened by her illness and shaken by the rituals she had seen, Zora was ready to leave Haiti.

She returned to America and hastily finished *Tell My Horse* in less than two months. Zora was in a hurry to put voodoo behind her. Her impatience to be done with the book shows—some of the writing is jumbled, and there are no footnotes or index.

Nevertheless, *Tell My Horse* is a fascinating account of West Indies life. By exploring the folk customs of Jamaica and Haiti, Zora helped dispel the notion that blacks had no culture of their own. She gave African-American culture a dignity that few others were willing to recognize at that time.

One of the most powerful sections of *Tell My Horse* is "Zombies." Zora describes her visit to a Haitian hospital, where she photographed a zombie. "It was a tremendous thrill," she remembered, "though utterly macabre." Did she see an actual zombie? Zora the anthropologist, who couldn't believe her own eyes, offers

the reader a scientific explanation. But Zora the partici-
pant, who was always transformed by her collecting experiences, flatly declares, "People have been called
back from the dead."

ZOMBIES

No one can stay in Haiti long without hearing
Zombies mentioned in one way or another, and
the fear of this thing and all that it means seeps
over the country like a ground current of cold air.
This fear is real and deep. It is more like a group of
fears.

For there is the outspoken fear among the peas-
ants of the work of Zombies. Sit in the market
place and pass a day with the market woman and
notice how often some vendeuse [vendor] cries out
that a Zombie with its invisible hand has filched
her money, or her goods. Or the accusation is
made that a Zombie has been set upon her or
some one of her family to work a piece of evil.

Big Zombies who come in the night to do malice
are talked about. Also the little girl Zombies who
are sent out by their owners in the dark dawn to
sell little packets of roasted coffee. Before sun up
their cries of "Café grillé" can be heard from dark
places in the streets and one can only see them if
one calls out for the seller to come with her goods.
Then the little dead one makes herself visible and
mounts the steps.

The upper class Haitians fear too, but they do not talk about it too openly as do the poor. But to them also it is a horrible possibility. Yet in spite of this obvious fear and the preparations that I found being made to safeguard the bodies of the dead against this possibility, I was told by numerous upper class Haitians that the whole thing was a myth. They pointed out that the common people were superstitious, and that the talk of Zombies had no more basis in fact than the European belief in the Werewolf.

But I had the good fortune to learn of several celebrated cases in the past and then in addition, I had the rare opportunity to see and touch an authentic case. I listened to the broken noises in its throat, and then, I did what no one else had ever done, I photographed it. If I had not experienced all of this in the strong sunlight of a hospital yard, I might have come away from Haiti interested but doubtful. But I saw this case of Felicia Felix-Mentor which was vouched for by the highest authority. So I know that there are Zombies in Haiti. People have been called back from the dead.

THE CASE OF FELICIA FELIX-MENTOR

We found the Zombie in the hospital yard. They had just set her dinner before her but she was not eating. She hovered against the fence in a sort of defensive position. The moment that she sensed our approach, she broke off a limb of a shrub and began to use it to dust and clean the ground and the fence and the table which bore her food. She huddled the cloth about her head more closely and showed every sign of fear and expectation of abuse and violence. The two doctors with me made kindly noises and tried to reassure her. She seemed to hear nothing. Just kept on trying to hide herself. The doctor uncovered her head for a moment but she promptly clapped her arms and hands over it to shut out the things she dreaded.

I said to the doctor that I had permission to take some pictures and he helped me to go about it. I took her first in the position that she assumed herself whenever left alone. That is cringing against the wall with the cloth hiding her face and head. Then in other positions. Finally the doctor forcibly uncovered her and held her so that I could take her face. And the sight was dreadful. That blank face with the dead eyes. The eyelids were white all around the eyes as if they had been burned with acid. It was pronounced enough to come out in the picture. There was nothing that you could say to her or get from her except by looking at her, and the sight of this wreckage was too much to endure for long.

Her name is Felicia Felix-Mentor. She and her husband kept a little grocery. She had one child, a boy. In 1907 she took suddenly ill and died and was buried. There were the records to show. The years passed. The husband married again and advanced himself in life. The little boy became a man. People had forgotten all about the wife and mother who had died so long ago.

Then one day in October 1936 someone saw a

naked woman on the road and reported it to the Garde d'Haiti [police]. Then this same woman turned up on a farm and said, "This is the farm of my father. I used to live here." The tenants tried to drive her away. Finally the boss was sent for and he came and recognized her as his sister who had died and been buried twenty-nine years before. She was in such wretched condition that the authorities were called in and she was sent to the hospital. Her husband was sent for to confirm the identification, but he refused. He was embarrassed by the matter as he was now a minor official and wanted nothing to do with the affair at all. But he was forced to come. He did so and reluctantly made the identification of this woman as his former wife.

How did this woman, supposedly dead for twenty-nine years, come to be wandering naked on a road? Nobody will tell who knows. The secret is with some bocor [magician] dead or alive. Sometimes a missionary converts one of these bocors and he gives up all his paraphernalia to the church and frees his captives if he has any. They are not freed publicly, you understand, as that would bring down the vengeance of the community upon his head. These creatures, unable to tell anything—for almost always they have lost the power of speech forever, are found wandering about. Sometimes the bocor dies and his widow refuses their responsibility for various reasons. Then again they are set free. Neither of these happenings is common.

Zora's photograph of Felicia Felix-Mentor, taken in Haiti in 1936. *Courtesy the Zora Neale Hurston Estate*

The doctor and I discussed at great length the theories of how Zombies come to be. It was concluded that it is not a case of awakening the dead, but a matter of the semblance of death induced by some drug known to a few. Some secret probably brought from Africa and handed down from generation to generation. These men know the effect of the drug and the antidote. It is evident that it destroys that part of the brain which governs speech and will power. The victims can move and act but cannot formulate thought. But the knowledge of the plants and formulae are secret. They are usually kept in certain families, and nothing will induce the guardians of these ancient mysteries to divulge them. Ah bo bo!

Zora's investigations were to pave the way for further research. In 1976, forty years after her trip to Haiti, scientists began to unravel the "ancient mysteries" of zombies. They now believe that zombies are victims of a poison made from the puffer fish. The poison is administered by secret voodoo sects as punishment for unacceptable social behavior, such as revealing voodoo secrets.

The zombie powder is inhaled or enters the body through a break in the skin. It causes complete paralysis. Although the victim remains conscious, he or she cannot move in any way and, by all appearances, is dead. Mourned and buried by the family, the victim is unearthed by the secret sect on the third night after burial and force-fed a paste made from a plant called the "zombie cucumber." (Not all potential zombies survive the poison or the three-day burial.)

The paste acts as an antidote, allowing the victim to "rise from the dead" and move about. But the antidote itself contains a powerful ingredient that causes confusion and amnesia. Already half-mad from the burial, the suffering victim is now psychotic. The zombification process is complete when he or she is beaten, given a new name, and forced into slavery—a poor soul doomed to a life of captivity or aimless wandering about the Haitian countryside. The victim has joined the "living dead."

Zombies are a far cry from the ghoulish Hollywood image portrayed in movies. They are helpless creatures incapable of caring for themselves, with little or no memory of their past lives. Worst of all to the Haitians, they have lost their "ti bon ange," or identity. Thus, a Haitian's greatest fear is not of being attacked by a zombie, but of becoming one.

By exploring the secret societies of Haiti, Zora uncovered valuable information that later led to the discovery of the zombie poison and its antidote. As she foretold, ". . . if science ever gets to the bottom of Voodoo in Haiti and Africa, it will be found that some important medical secrets, still unknown to medical science, give it its power, rather than the gestures of ceremony." Zora's pioneer exploration of zombies helped to make her own predictions come true.

◆ 10 ◆

NEW YORK

When Zora left New York for her first trip to Haiti, she left behind a stormy romance that was "the real love affair" of her life. She never revealed his full name, for Zora was intensely private about her personal life. A. W. P., as she called him in her autobiography, was a handsome, intelligent man of West Indian ancestry.

Zora fell deeply in love, but, as with her first husband, she was torn between her writing and a man who wanted a wife to stay home and love only him. She was in a difficult position. Zora had been shocked to hear a Jamaican man contend that "American women were destroyed by their brains." Now she loved someone who begged her to give up her career—to stop using her brains.

A lack of trust made matters worse between the two lovers. If Zora had to meet with her publisher, A. W. P. begged her not to go. If he smiled at another woman, Zora was furious. She described their relationship as "an agonizing tug of war." Finally, she decided to end the jealous quarrels. The offer of the Guggenheim Fellowship made the painful decision easier. By continuing her research, she could "release him and fight myself free."

Grieving over the broken affair, Zora wrote a love story in Haiti that is now considered her masterpiece: *Their Eyes Were Watching God*. In contrast to protest novels of the thirties, which carried a message about the misery of black life in America, *Their Eyes* revolves around a black woman's search for happiness. Zora's book leaves out the suffering, one critic has noted, and includes "the laughter and loving that are a part of Black life."

Janie Crawford is the main character of the book. She is raised by a grandmother who wants her to "pick from a higher bush and a sweeter berry." Her granny says that "[d]e nigger woman is de mule of de world," and she insists that Janie marry an older man who will protect her from abuse. Janie agrees to the marriage, but it is an empty arrangement. When she discovers that "marriage could not compel love like the sun the day," she leaves her husband for Joe Starks.

Joe takes Janie to a fictional Eatonville, where he becomes mayor and starts a store. The romance fades as Joe dominates Janie with his powerful personality. He forces her to keep her hair covered by a kerchief and to work long hours at the store. Worst of all, he refuses to let Janie have her say or to listen to her opinions.

Twenty years with Joe "took all the fight out of Janie's face." Only after his death does Janie find fulfillment with a man. Vergible "Tea Cake" Woods is fifteen years younger than Janie, but he makes her laugh. More important, he is strong enough to love her and let her be herself at the same time.

Zora claimed that the plot of *Their Eyes Were Watching God* was "far from the circumstances" of her love affair with A. W. P. She did admit to putting "all the tenderness of my passion" for him into the book, and Zora's A. W. P. does resemble Janie's Tea Cake. They both possess good looks, physical strength, and a great capacity for love.

In this chapter from *Their Eyes Were Watching God*, Zora reveals through Janie both the jealousy and the joy of her own love for A. W. P. Janie and Tea Cake have moved to the Florida Everglades. Along with other migrant workers, they have come for the season to pick beans. The two lovers are wildly happy—until Janie sees Tea Cake with another woman.

JEALOUSY

Janie learned what it felt like to be jealous. A little chunky girl took to picking a play out of Tea Cake in the fields and in the quarters. If he said anything at all, she'd take the opposite side and hit him or shove him and run away to make him chase her. Janie knew what she was up to—luring him away from the crowd. It kept up for two or three weeks with Nunkie getting bolder all the time. She'd hit Tea Cake playfully and the minute he so much as tapped her with his finger she'd fall against him or fall on the ground and have to be picked up. She'd be almost helpless. It took a good deal of handling to set her on her feet again. And another thing, Tea Cake didn't seem to be able to fend her off as promptly as Janie thought he ought to. She began to be snappish a little. A little seed of fear was growing into a tree. Maybe some day Tea Cake would weaken. Maybe he had already given secret encouragement and this was Nunkie's way of bragging about it. Other people began to notice too, and that put Janie more on a wonder.

One day they were working near where the beans ended and the sugar cane began. Janie had marched off a little from Tea Cake's side with another woman for a chat. When she glanced around Tea Cake was gone. Nunkie too. She knew because she looked.

"Where's Tea Cake?" she asked Sop-de-Bottom.

He waved his hand towards the cane field and hurried away. Janie never thought at all. She just acted on feelings. She rushed into the cane and about the fifth row down she found Tea Cake and Nunkie struggling. She was on them before either knew.

"Whut's de matter heah?" Janie asked in a cold rage. They sprang apart.

"Nothin'," Tea Cake told her, standing shame-faced.

"Well, whut you doin' in heah? How come you ain't out dere wid de rest?"

"She grabbed mah workin' tickets outa mah shirt

pocket and Ah run tuh git 'em back," Tea Cake explained, showing the tickets, considerably mauled about in the struggle.

Janie made a move to seize Nunkie but the girl fled. So she took out behind her over the humped-up cane rows. But Nunkie did not mean to be caught. So Janie went on home. The sight of the fields and the other happy people was too much for her that day. She walked slowly and thoughtfully to the quarters. It wasn't long before Tea Cake found her there and tried to talk. She cut him short with a blow and they fought from one room to the other, Janie trying to beat him, and Tea Cake kept holding her wrists and wherever he could to keep her from going too far.

"Ah b'lieve you been messin' round her!" she panted furiously.

"No sich uh thing!" Tea Cake retorted.

"Ah b'lieve yuh did."

"Don't keer how big uh lie get told, somebody kin b'lieve it!"

They fought on. "You done hurt mah heart, now you come wid uh lie tuh bruise mah ears! Turn go mah hands!" Janie seethed. But Tea Cake never let go. They wrestled on until they were doped with their own fumes and emanations; till their clothes had been torn away; till he hurled her to the floor and held her there melting her resistance with the heat of his body, doing things with their bodies to express the inexpressible; kissed her until she arched her body to meet him and they fell asleep in sweet exhaustion.

The next morning Janie asked like a woman, "You still love ole Nunkie?"

"Naw, never did, and you know it too. Ah didn't want her."

"Yeah, you did." She didn't say this because she believed it. She wanted to hear his denial. She had to crow over the fallen Nunkie.

"Whut would Ah do wid dat lil chunk of a woman wid you around? She ain't good for nothin' exceptin' tuh set up in uh corner by de kitchen stove and break wood over her head. You'se something tuh make uh man forgit tuh git old and forgit tuh die."

◆ 11 ◆

DUST TRACKS

Zora's career reached its peak in the thirties. She published five books in that decade, including *Moses, Man of the Mountain*, a black version of the biblical story of Moses. By 1939, her creative efforts had passed those of any other black woman writer, and no other writer had done as much to promote the cultural heritage of black Americans. Single-handedly, Zora Neale Hurston had presented black culture in a readable form for a popular audience.

But by then, her artistic differences with other black writers were clearly defined. When *Their Eyes Were Watching God* was published in 1937, white critics hailed Zora's accurate portrayal of Negro speech. Comments from her black colleagues, however, were negative. Alain Locke, Ralph Ellison, and Richard Wright disliked her portrayal of blacks as common folks working in the bean fields.

Wright had grown up in poverty on a Mississippi

A woodcut Christmas card from Zora to Ralph Hartman, 1940. The card is an example of how Zora's sense of humor could both entertain and offend. The verse is exuberant, but the picture is a caricature. It was typical of her to nullify the power of racism by making fun of it. *Courtesy McBlain Books, Hampden, Connecticut, and the Zora Neale Hurston Estate*

plantation. Like Zora, he left home at an early age and worked at low-paying jobs. Eventually he became a writer, and his bitter memories of sweeping streets and digging ditches shaped his fiction. As editor of *The New Challenge* magazine, Wright issued a call to all black authors to describe the horrors of racism—to hold up a mirror so white America could see its own cruelty.

Because he considered writing a political tool, Wright thought that the story of Janie Crawford was a wasted one. It did nothing to wake up the country to inequality. Zora's characters were too simple. They "eat and laugh and cry and work and kill . . ." he said, criticizing her book for its "minstrel image."

Zora felt that Wright's viewpoint was narrow. In 1938 she reviewed his first book, *Uncle Tom's Children*. She resented his portrayal of the South as a "dismal, hopeless section ruled by brutish hatred and nothing else." Wright's novel of a Chicago ghetto, *Native Son*, was published in 1940. Zora gave it grudging praise, but she thought it was bleak.

"Yes, I think *Native Son* is a swell book," she wrote to a friend. "A trifle gloomy, and to me it does not follow as the night the day that the hero had to come out that way because of the national set-up. There are too many successful Negroes in America to take that stand. However, it is most beautifully written and cracks like machine-gun fire." Zora was a stubborn optimist about American blacks; Wright was a determined realist. Both writers had grown up in the rural South, but they were worlds apart in purpose and style.

Zora Neale Hurston and Richard Wright are now seen as equally brilliant authors with powerful, if different, visions of black life. But during the Depression years, it was Wright's tale of despair that matched the mood of the country, not Zora's story of black love. *Native Son* was chosen by the Book-of-the-Month Club, was made into a movie, and sold three hundred thousand copies. *Their Eyes Were Watching God* went out of print before it sold five thousand copies. By the early forties, Zora was out of step creatively with other black writers, and she was out of money.

In 1942, critics blasted Zora once again, this time for her autobiography, *Dust Tracks on a Road*. Arna Bontemps, a black poet, said she ignored the "serious aspects of Negro life in America." A review in the *Journal of Negro History* accused Zora of recycling folk material from her previous books. A white critic, Harold Preece, called her autobiography the "tragedy of a gifted mind." Fortunately for her strained finances, the book was praised by New York critics and won a thousand-dollar race-relations award. But to achieve this recognition, she had to tread lightly on the toes of white readers.

Zora skipped over any discussion of racial discrimination. She barely mentioned the Harlem Renaissance, glossed over Jim Crow laws, and even distorted her treatment as the only black in her class at Barnard. "The *Social Register* crowd at Barnard soon took me up," she bragged, but she failed to mention that she was not allowed to attend the prom.

Zora had found a recipe for success and badly needed royalty checks—entertain, but don't blame. Some of her autobiography sounds false, partly because she wrote it with a white audience in mind, partly because she was a private person. "I was not happy to write it," she said in a letter. "It is much too personal to suit me. My publishers insisted."

Also, parts of *Dust Tracks* seem artificial because Zora insisted that the cup of black life was full. She had led a protected childhood in all-black Eatonville. To Zora, being black was a joy, not a cross to bear. She liked herself and her color. No black could completely avoid the barriers of a segregated America, but her strong sense of self allowed her to rise above the indignities of prejudice. One example shows how she ignored discrimination.

In 1942, she taught part-time at the Florida Normal School, a black college in Saint Augustine, Florida. She asked Marjorie Kinnan Rawlings, author of *The Yearling,* to be a guest speaker for her class. Rawlings then invited Zora to tea at her home: a segregated hotel owned by her husband. Rather than ride the elevator, Zora chose to enter through the kitchen and go up the stairs.

The tea was a success. Rawlings recalled that Zora was a "lush, fine-looking café-au-lait person," and was impressed by her "brilliant mind" and "superb work." Although she privately worried that accepting Zora "as a human being and a friend" might hurt her husband's business, the two writers eventually became close. Rawlings developed a fondness for Zora, who thought that Marjorie Kinnan Rawlings was "good and kind to everybody."

Five years later, that back-door visit helped Zora publish what would be her last book. Rawlings put Zora in touch with her own editor at Scribners, who bought

the option for her next novel. Zora's critics have wondered how she could tolerate racial humiliation and enjoy her white friendships at the same time. But in both
her personal life and *Dust Tracks,* she chose to "just
see people" and not the race problems in America. If
her color had been an obstacle in her life, she refused
to admit it publicly in her autobiography.

Zora did not identify with what she called "the sob-
bing school of Negrohood," a stance that was costly in
the long run. Throughout the forties and fifties, her
opinions on race would often be misinterpreted, especially when she opposed the 1954 Supreme Court decision to integrate schools. Zora thought the ruling was
insulting to black teachers and that black students were
perfectly capable of learning, even if they didn't sit be-
side whites.

"The whole matter revolves around the self-respect
of my people," she wrote in a letter to the editor of the
Orlando Sentinel. "How much satisfaction can I get
from a court order for somebody to associate with me
who does not wish me to be near them?" Blacks were
outraged by Zora's views on what she called "the segregation mess," but the letter only preached what she had
practiced all her life. When Fannie Hurst, her employer in the early Harlem years, had tried to integrate
a white hotel with Zora in tow, Zora refused to follow.
"This is the way it is," she insisted, ". . . I can take care
of myself as I have all my life." So Zora found her own
lodging—after all, how could staying under the same
roof as white folks improve a good night's sleep?

Zora's racial pride was years ahead of the black sepa-
ratist movement of the sixties—a time when black

would be beautiful. Instead, she was considered disloyal by her black contemporaries, who were fighting to be part of the mainstream of American life. She was known more as a discredit to her race than as a writer, a reputation that blurred her accomplishments for years to come.

"High John the Conquer"* was originally written as a patriotic essay for a white magazine, *American Mercury*. It is one of the few pieces of folklore that Zora published in the forties. Perhaps with the color of her readers in mind, she avoided direct accusations of racism. Instead, this story gently reminded her white audience of the cruelties of slavery.

The story tells the origin of John, a mythical folk character who appears in many black American folktales. John brought humor, wisdom, and power to the slaves. His strength was so great that conjure doctors named a root after him. High John the Conquer root was used to cure many ills and to bring good luck, especially in court cases.

HIGH JOHN THE CONQUER

High John the Conquer came to be a man, and a mighty man at that. But he was not a natural man in the beginning. First off, he was a whisper, a will to hope, a wish to find something worthy of laughter and song. Then the whisper put on flesh. His

---

*Zora used the dialectical spelling.

footsteps sounded across the world in a low but musical rhythm as if the world he walked on was a singing-drum. The black folks had an irresistible impulse to laugh. High John the Conquer was a man in full, and had come to live and work on the plantations, and all the slave folks knew him in the flesh.

The sign of this man was a laugh, and his singing-symbol was a drumbeat. No parading drum-shout like soldiers out for show. It did not call to the feet of those who were fixed to it. It was an inside thing to live by. It was sure to be heard when and where the work was the hardest, and the lot the most cruel. It helped the slaves endure.

They knew that something better was coming. So they laughed in the face of things and sang, "I'm so glad! Trouble don't last always." And the white people who heard them were struck dumb that they could laugh.

Old Massa couldn't know of course, but High John the Conquer was there walking his plantation like a natural man. He was treading the sweat-flavored clods of the plantation, crushing out his drum tunes, and giving out secret laughter. He walked on the winds and moved fast. Maybe he was in Texas when the lash fell on a slave in Alabama, but before the blood was dry on the back he was there.

A faint pulsing of a drum like a goatskin stretched over a heart, that came nearer and closer, then somebody in the saddened quarters would feel like laughing, and say, "Now, High John de Conquer, Old Massa couldn't get the best of *him*. That old John was a case!" Then everybody sat up and began to smile. Yes, yes, that was right. Old John, High John could beat the unbeatable. He was top-superior to the whole mess of sorrow. He could beat it all, and what made it so cool, finish it off with a laugh.

So they pulled the covers up over their souls and kept them from all hurt, harm and danger and made them a laugh and a song. Night time was a joke, because daybreak was on the way. Distance and the impossible had no power over High John the Conquer.

He had come from Africa. He came walking on the waves of sound. Then he took on flesh after he got here. The sea captains of ships knew that they brought slaves in their ships. They knew about those black bodies huddled down there in the middle passage, being hauled across the waters to helplessness. John the Conquer was walking the very winds that filled the sails of the ships. He followed over them like the albatross.

There is no established picture of what sort of looking-man this John the Conquer was. To some, he was a big, physical-looking man like John Henry. To others, he was a little, hammered-down, low-built man like the Devil's doll-baby. Some said that they never heard what he looked like. Nobody told them, but he lived on the plantation where their old folks were slaves. He is not so well known to the present generation of colored people in the same way that he was in slavery time.

Like King Arthur of England, he has served his people, and gone back into mystery again. And, like King Arthur, he is not dead. He waits to return when his people shall call again. Symbolic of English power, Arthur came out of the water, and with his sword Excalibur, went back into the water again. High John the Conquer went back to Africa, but he left his power here, and placed his American dwelling in the root of a certain plant. Only possess that root, and he can be summoned at any time.

◆ 12 ◆
FLORIDA

During the early forties, Zora lived alone on a houseboat in Florida. The solitude and independence of living on the river brought her contentment, despite growing health and financial problems.

Zora had suffered from intestinal attacks for years. At one point, she even sat on an inner tube to ease the pain as she watched rehearsal of one of her plays. Zora had a knack for making the best of a bad situation—it's easy to imagine her cracking jokes and making light of her position in an inner tube.

It's not so easy to imagine writing books while living with chronic pain year after year. By 1945, she had ulcers and wrote a friend, "I have been sick with my colon and general guts for a long, long time . . . for a while I thought I would kick the bucket."

Often sick and always short of money, Zora steadfastly pursued her career. During the forties, she published twenty-one articles and wrote two books. One of the books was rejected by her publisher. Zora's writing had begun to slip. She had drifted away from the folklore that had made her previous books so remarkable, although her last published book, *Seraph on the Suwanee,* received good reviews.

In 1948, the same year *Seraph* was published, Zora was involved in a scandal that left her in despair. In New York, the mother of a ten-year-old mentally disturbed boy falsely accused Zora of sexually molesting her son. Zora was collecting folklore in Central America at the time. Despite proof that she had been out of the country, the police believed the mother's story. Zora was arrested and indicted. Appalled, she blamed an "anti-Negro" sentiment in the courts for allowing the case to progress so far.

Zora was cleared of all charges, but not before a black newspaper printed the accusations in a front-page story. "Novelist Arrested on Morals Charge," the sensational headlines of the *Baltimore Afro-American* read. Quoting from *Seraph,* the paper accused Zora of being "hungry as a dog for . . . love."

She felt attacked from all sides. Worse than persecution by the white legal system was betrayal by the black press. The *Afro-American* exploited Zora's case for commercial reasons, as the paper clearly used tabloid journalism to sell copies. Another headline on the same page read, "Police Seeking Bathtub Killer of Young Mother."

But there was also an element of punishment. Zora had expressed views that were unpopular in the black community. She was an "uppity" educated woman with a career—fair game for a newspaper controlled by black

Zora (*center*) in Florida in the late 1950s. The photograph was damaged by fire after her death. *Courtesy Department of Rare Books and Manuscripts, University of Florida Library*

men. Her depression over the scandal eventually lifted, but it left her bitter. She felt her reputation was ruined. "My country has failed me utterly," she wrote. "My race has seen fit to destroy me without reason. . . ."

To recover from the scandal that "knocked me loose from all that I have ever looked to and cherished," Zora returned to the Florida sunshine. An earlier trip to Honduras to search for folklore had been cut short by lack of funds. In Miami, she hoped to gather enough money to try again.

Incredibly, at fifty-eight, Zora was ready for a new

adventure. Snakes, fevers, and hostile Indians were nothing compared to the excitement of discovering pagan rites performed by the descendants of a lost Mayan civilization. The "awe" and "terror" of the unexplored jungles of Central America didn't dampen Zora's curiosity, but lack of money did. Although her efforts to finance the trip were unsuccessful, she managed to put the New York disgrace behind her.

In 1950, Zora Hurston made the papers once more. When she went to work as a maid for thirty dollars a week, headlines in the *Miami Herald* read, "Famous Negro Author Working as Maid Here Just to Live a Little." Zora's explanation, "A change of pace is good for everyone," barely covered her desperate need for work.

By 1951, she was living with friends but longed to live alone again. She wrote to a friend, "Just inching along like a stepped-on worm from day to day. Borrowing a little here and there."

When a published article brought in one thousand dollars, Zora rented the same cabin in Eau Gallie, Florida, where twenty years earlier she had written *Mules and Men*. Her letters show that the next five years were tranquil ones. Only two blocks from the "world's most beautiful river," Zora turned the one-room cabin into a home. She planted pink verbena and used a nearby artesian well to set up a fountain.

In 1956, the cabin was sold, and Zora was forced to move on. She worked as a librarian, earning $1.88 an hour, but the job ended when her supervisor found her overqualified for the job. Living on a weekly $26 unemployment check, she moved to a house trailer on an island off Cocoa, Florida. C. E. Bolen, owner of a weekly black newspaper in Fort Pierce, visited the island in December 1957. After meeting Zora, he offered her a room in his home and a job as a free-lance writer for the paper.

Zora contributed to the *Fort Pierce Chronicle* for the next two years, writing horoscopes and a column called "Hoodoo and Black Magic." Bolen remembers her as an energetic intellectual, forced by lack of money to "live roughly." She had "spots on her dress," he recalls, but "her real value was in her brain." She was also not the easiest guest to have around. "She could cuss you out in a nice way," Bolen said, "and you would never know what she was talking about. She was something with those words. . . ."

Bolen's house was across the street from Lincoln Park Academy, the black public school in Fort Pierce. In February 1958, Zora began substituting as an English teacher, earning the usual low substitute pay. "She lived a different life than a lot of people," remembered Margaret Paige, an administrator at the school. "She just didn't seem to care about things the way the rest of us did—about a comfortable place to live, nice clothes, that kind of thing. She was just different."

She was also poor. But despite the poverty, her writing remained a priority. Zora continued to work on a book she had begun in Eau Gallie, a biography of Herod the Great. Although the manuscript was rejected by two publishers, she clung to her belief that Herod's life would make "a great story."

Sixty-seven-year-old Zora was without a publisher, without funds, and in failing health. She was overweight (she loved to eat "mounds and mounds of ice cream"), had high blood pressure, and suffered from an ulcer and gall bladder attacks. At a time when she should have been enjoying the fruits of a thirty-year writing career, she was unable to rely on royalties or even a pension.

Zora herself admitted that she had no stomach for money matters. "I was in the midst of a business squabble," she once said of a contract dispute, ". . . and it was crushing me like a mountain falling on a milk cow."

Zora was not known for having good money sense, but that is a difficult skill to learn when there is so little money to manage. The most carefully planned budget could not have stretched 24¢, all she had to her name when forced to return from collecting in the Bahamas. On the day one of her books was accepted, she was being evicted from a rented room for $18 rent. The largest royalty check Zora ever received from a publisher was $943.75. Outside of writing, she never had a job for more than a year.

Perhaps if there had been a larger black reading public, or if southern bookstores had not refused to carry her books, Zora might not have ended up, as she put it, "cold in hand," a folk term for being broke. It has been said that "Writing is the only profession where no one considers you ridiculous if you earn no money." For Zora Hurston, this was painfully true.

Zora spent the last years of her life in a rent-free concrete blockhouse owned by her physician, Dr. C. C. Benton. Her spirit remained unbreakable. She planted flowers and a vegetable garden, and entertained the neighborhood children with stories. She loved jazz, and often went to hear jazz trumpet and piano played at local jam sessions. One friend remembered that when Zora came to visit, she told tales and slapped her large feet down for comic effect—she still had the ability to "make you laugh one minute and cry the next."

She depended on her doctor for companionship, an occasional meal, and groceries. "Come over here and see 'bout me," she would say to him when she felt too sick to go out for food.

"She was an incredible woman," Benton recalled. "She was always studying. Her mind—before the stroke—just worked all the time." Even after a stroke early in 1959, Zora wrote when she could. Her last newspaper column is dated August 7, 1959, just two months before she entered the St. Lucie County welfare home. She balked at going in the home, but already dependent on welfare for food and medicine, she had no choice.

Out of pride, Zora did not notify relatives of her condition. Friends visited, bringing books and magazines for her to read, and one of them remembers that Zora was always cheerful. She wasn't a person to "let things get her down," he said. She always thought that "everything was going to get better."

Zora died of heart disease on the night of January 28, 1960. The burial was delayed for ten days while friends raised $600 to pay for funeral expenses, including $2.50 in change donated by former students. One hundred people attended the service held at the funeral home. Seniors from Lincoln Park Academy served as flower girls, and faculty members as pallbearers. She was bur-

ied in a bronze metallic casket in a segregated cemetery. Bushes and weeds were the only grave marker for
Zora Neale Hurston, one of the notable writers of this
century.

> I know that nothing is destructible; things merely
> change forms. When the consciousness we know as
> life ceases, I know that I shall still be part and parcel
> of the world. I was a part before the sun rolled into
> shape and burst forth in the glory of change. I was,
> when the earth was hurled out from its fiery rim. I
> shall return with the earth to Father Sun, and still
> exist in substance when the sun has lost its fire, and
> disintegrated in infinity to perhaps become a part of
> the whirling rubble in space. Why fear? The stuff of
> my being is matter, ever changing, ever moving, but
> never lost. . . .
>
> Zora Neale Hurston, *Dust Tracks on a Road*

Alice Walker, author of *The Color Purple,* has helped
restore Zora's rightful place as an important literary figure. In 1973, Walker traveled to south Florida to put a
stone on Zora's unmarked grave.

The following excerpt is from her essay "Looking for
Zora." Walker, pretending to be Zora's niece, has just
left the funeral home that had buried Zora thirteen
years earlier. She sets out to find Zora's grave, accompanied by a friend, Charlotte, and an employee of the
funeral home, Rosalee.

LOOKING FOR ZORA

"What is your name?" I ask the woman who has climbed into the back seat.

"Rosalee," she says. She has a rough, pleasant voice, as if she is a singer who also smokes a lot. She is homely, and has an air of ready indifference.

"Another woman came by here wanting to see the grave," she says, lighting up a cigarette. "She was a little short, dumpty white lady from one of these Florida schools. Orlando or Daytona. But let me tell you something before we gets started. All I know is where the cemetery is. I don't know one thing about that grave. You better go back in and ask her to draw you a map."

A few moments later, with Mrs. Patterson's diagram of where the grave is, we head for the cemetery.

We drive past blocks of small, pastel-colored houses and turn right onto 17th Street. At the very end, we reach a tall curving gate, with the words "Garden of the Heavenly Rest" fading into the stone. I expected, from Mrs. Patterson's small drawing, to find a small circle—which would have placed Zora's grave five or ten paces from the road. But the "circle" is over an acre large and looks more like an abandoned field. Tall weeds choke the dirt road and scrape against the sides of the car. It doesn't help either that I step out into an active anthill.

"I don't know about y'all," I say, "but I don't even believe this." I am used to the haphazard

cemetery-keeping that is traditional in most Southern black communities, but this neglect is stagger-
ing. As far as I can see there is nothing but bushes
and weeds, some as tall as my waist. One grave is
near the road, and Charlotte elects to investigate
it. It is fairly clean, and belongs to someone who
died in 1963.

Rosalee and I plunge into the weeds; I pull my
long dress up to my hips. The weeds scratch my
knees, and the insects have a feast. Looking back,
I see Charlotte standing resolutely near the road.

"Aren't you coming?" I call.

"No," she calls back. "I'm from these parts and I
know what's out there." She means snakes.

"Shit," I say, my whole life and the people I love
flashing melodramatically before my eyes. Rosalee
is a few yards to my right.

"How're you going to find anything out here?"
she asks. And I stand still a few seconds, looking at
the weeds. Some of them are quite pretty, with
tiny yellow flowers. They are thick and healthy,
but dead weeds under them have formed a thick
gray carpet on the ground. A snake could be lying
six inches from my big toe and I wouldn't see it.
We move slowly, very slowly, our eyes alert, our
legs trembly. It is hard to tell where the center of
the circle is since the circle is not really round, but
more like half of something round. There are
things crackling and hissing in the grass. Sand-
spurs are sticking to the inside of my skirt. Sand
and ants cover my feet. I look toward the road and
notice that there are, indeed, *two* large curving

stones, making an entrance and exit to the cemetery. I take my bearings from them and try to navi-
gate to exact center. But the center of anything
can be very large, and a grave is not a pinpoint.
Finding the grave seems positively hopeless.
There is only one thing to do:

"Zora!" I yell, as loud as I can (causing Rosalee
to jump), "are you out here?"

"If she is, I sho hope she don't answer you. If
she do, I'm gone."

"Zora!" I call again. "I'm here. Are you?"

"If she is," grumbles Rosalee, "I hope she'll
keep it to herself."

"Zora!" Then I start fussing with her. "I hope
you don't think I'm going to stand out here all day,
with these snakes watching me and these ants having a field day. In fact, I'm going to call you just
one or two more times." On a clump of dried
grass, near a small bushy tree, my eye falls on one
of the largest bugs I have ever seen. It is on its
back, and is as large as three of my fingers. I walk
toward it, and yell "Zo-ra!" and my foot sinks into
a hole. I look down. I am standing in a sunken
rectangle that is about six feet long and about
three or four feet wide. I look up to see where the
two gates are.

"Well," I say, "this is the center, or approx-
imately anyhow. It's also the only sunken spot
we've found. Doesn't this look like a grave to
you?"

"For the sake of not going no farther through
these bushes," Rosalee growls, "yes, it do."

"Wait a minute," I say, "I have to look around some more to be sure this is the only spot that resembles a grave. But you don't have to come."

Rosalee smiles—a grin, really—beautiful and tough.

"Naw," she says, "I feels sorry for you. If one of these snakes got ahold of you out here by yourself I'd feel *real* bad." She laughs. "I done come this far, I'll go on with you."

"Thank you, Rosalee," I say. "Zora thanks you too."

"Just as long as she don't try to tell me in person," she says, and together we walk down the field.

A light gray stone now marks Zora's grave in the Garden of Heavenly Rest in Fort Pierce, Florida. The weeds are cleared annually, and local members of Zeta Phi Beta sorority visit the site to leave flowers in her memory. The words that Alice Walker chose for the headstone sum up her accomplishments: novelist, folklorist, anthropologist. But beyond these achievements lies a remarkable spirit.

Zora sought independence when southern black women, only a few generations removed from slavery, were expected to be subservient. She fought for an education—in 1920, as legislators argued whether women were smart enough to vote, she was putting herself through college. In a day when success was measured by the number of children a woman had produced, she

Zora Neale Hurston's grave in Fort Pierce, Florida, summer 1989. "I have been in Sorrow's Kitchen. . . . I have licked out all the pots." (*Zora Neale Hurston*, Dust Tracks on a Road). *Courtesy Juan Dale Brown*

chose a career. Despite incredible odds, Zora Neale Hurston made her own luck. "I shall wrassle me up a future," she once said, "or die trying."

Zora was an adventurer. She climbed mountains and explored jungles in search of folklore, and thought nothing of taking her houseboat from Florida to New York—a fifteen hundred-mile journey by sea. She was a rebel, who once spoke to a group of GI's in World War II and surprised them by wearing an outfit seldom seen on a woman in the forties—pants and a leather vest.

In a time of few divorces, Zora Neale Hurston was a radical. Her second marriage was as brief as her first: only eight months, and to a man twenty-five years younger than she. She was a loner, but vulnerable to loneliness. After the breakup of her second marriage, she returned to New York and wrote to a friend, "Do write me a letter. . . . I feel strange and cold and a little afraid again."

Her critics called her a faker and a publicity seeker. Her admirers call her an artist and a pioneer. But perhaps the best way to describe Zora is that she was simply *herself*. "Zora would have been Zora," a friend once said, "even if she was an Eskimo."

Many years have passed since that May evening in 1925 when fifteen writers were honored at a banquet. Most of those authors are long forgotten. But thanks to the attention created by Alice Walker, and a biography written by Robert Hemenway, Zora is still with us. Six of her books have been reprinted, along with two collections of her short works.

Several plays have dramatized her life, and Eatonville residents honored her in their 1990 Zora Neale

Hurston Festival of the Arts. *Their Eyes Were Watching God* is featured in an American Library Association poster. There's even a Zora Neale Hurston T-shirt. For readers who enjoy folklore and admire an unsquinched spirit, the "little brown person" from Eatonville lives on.

AUTHOR'S NOTE

Writing about Zora Neale Hurston was a challenge, for there were many sides to her personality. It was difficult to see a clear image of Zora. Often it seemed that the more I learned about her, the less I knew.

Because her autobiography misleads the reader, it was especially hard to figure dates correctly. Sometimes I wanted to sit her down, bribe her with a bowl of ice cream, and sternly demand that she give an accurate account of her life. The cure for my frustration with Zora was Zora herself. I would reread one of her books (usually *Mules and Men*, but every Zora fan has her favorite), and the writing always amused or touched me.

The most interesting experience I had while researching her life was at the Library of Congress, where I listened to her voice on tape. To hear Zora describe a gambling game called Georgia Skin was an exciting moment for me. "My name is Zora Neale Hurston," I heard her say in an energetic voice. "Put the money on the wood and make the bet go good . . . put it in sight and save a fight!" She sounded strong, proud, and very southern.

Zora's writing and the sound of her voice kept me going, but without others, this book wouldn't have been written at all. I owe a debt to Alice Walker. Zora had been lost for years, and Walker found her for us. Robert Hemenway's book, *Zora Neale Hurston: A Literary Biography*, tells where she had been and how she got there. Hemenway invested eight years of travel and research in his book. No one can write about Zora without relying on his fine biography, for his contributions to the study of her life are invaluable.

Much of my information came from Zora's own works. My husband, a used- and rare-book dealer, provided many of the out-of-print sources that I needed and saved me countless trips to the library. That was fortunate, because Zora is so popular with scholars that some books and articles about her had been permanently "borrowed."

I am grateful to two people who knew Zora in Fort Pierce, Florida. Chester Bolen and A. E. Backus agreed to telephone interviews and helped me understand what life was like for her during her last years.

I called a number of libraries to find information on Zora, including those at Yale and Howard universities. Staff members were always helpful. The librarian from the St. Lucie County Library System in Fort Pierce, Florida, was particularly patient with my requests. As a writer, I believe that reference librarians are America's greatest resource.

The first group of people who helped me are, finally, the most important: the young people I have known as a teacher and librarian in the public schools. Their enthusiasm and curiosity confirmed my belief that young adults needed a "Zora book" of their own.

NOTES

Quotations not attributed are from Zora Neale Hurston's writings.

Preface

p. ix   CONSIDERED MASTERPIECES: Robert Hemenway, *Zora Neale Hurston: A Literary Biography*, p. 215.

p. x   ". . . WORSHIP STRENGTH": Zora Neale Hurston quoted by Stanley J. Kunitz, ed., *Twentieth-Century American Authors, First Supplement*, p. 695.

Chapter 1. HOME

p. 1   SHOCK THE LADIES: Zora Neale Hurston, "Zora Neale Hurston Writes About Herself," dust jacket from *Seraph on the Suwanee.*

p. 2   "WORKS OF THE DEVIL": *Ibid.* "BLOOD AND THUNDER": *Ibid.* ". . . POET LIKE LONGFELLOW": *Ibid.* ". . . BE A MISSIONARY": *Ibid.*

Chapter 2. EATONVILLE

p. 11   FEAR WHITE STRANGERS: Stanley J. Kunitz, *Twentieth-Century American Authors, First Supplement*, p. 695.

p. 11   SEVENTY-SEVEN LYNCHINGS: Peter M. Bergman, *The Chronological History of the Negro in America*.

p. 11   RURAL SOUTH: Charles Wesley, ed., *International Library of Afro-American Life and History*, p. 107.

p. 14–15 EXPLANATION OF EATONVILLE FOLK BELIEFS: Robert Hemenway, *Zora Neale Hurston*, p. 16.

Chapter 3. BALTIMORE AND WASHINGTON

p. 21   BORN IN 1891: Robert Hemenway, Introduction to *Dust Tracks on a Road*, p. xi.

p. 21   PROBABLY THIRTEEN: Robert Hemenway, *Zora Neale Hurston*, p. 32, note 8.

p. 21   SECRET MARRIAGE: *Ibid.*, p. 17.

p. 25   ELEVEN MILLION BLACKS, 67 BLACK PUBLIC HIGH SCHOOLS, 20,000 STUDENTS: *Fourteenth United States Census*, p. 1043.

p. 30   "ROUGH-EDGED DIAMOND": Robert Hemenway, *Zora Neale Hurston*, p. 18.

p. 32   *C* IF THEY WOULD NOT RETURN: David Levering Lewis, *When Harlem Was in Vogue*, p. 96.

Chapter 4. HARLEM I

p. 33   THE "GREAT MIGRATION": August Meier and Elliott Rudwick, *From Plantation to Ghetto*, p. 215.

p. 33   THREE HUNDRED THOUSAND BLACK WORKERS: David Levering Lewis, *When Harlem Was in Vogue*, p. 20.

p. 33   BOLL WEEVIL: Meier and Rudwick, p. 216.

p. 33   ONE-THIRD LESS MONEY: Lewis, p. 21.

p. 34   ". . . IN TWO WEEKS": T. Arnold Hill requoted by Lewis, p. 20.

p. 34   DOUBLING THE POPULATION OF NEW YORK CITY: Arnold Rampersad, *The Life of Langston Hughes, Volume I*, p. 51.

p. 34   GEORGIA, THE CAROLINAS, VIRGINIA: Lewis, 27.

p. 35   DESCRIPTION OF AWARDS DINNER: *Opportunity*, 3:29 (25 May 1925): 142–43.

p. 35   ". . . WOULD LIKE TO KNOW HER": Langston Hughes

requoted by Rampersad, *The Life of Langston Hughes, Volume I*, p. 107.

p. 35 ". . . BEST AND THE BRIGHTEST": Alain Locke requoted by Lewis, p. 96.

p. 35 "NEW SOUL": Alain Locke, Introduction to *The New Negro: An Interpretation*, p. xi.

p. 37 ". . . DOWN TO A FOOTSTOOL": Langston Hughes, *The Langston Hughes Reader*, p. 378.

p. 37 "BLAZING ZEST FOR LIFE": Fannie Hurst requoted by Robert Hemenway, *Zora Neale Hurston*, p. 21.

p. 37 ". . . EVERYTHING AT ONCE": Zora Neale Hurston requoted *Ibid.*, p. 23.

p. 37 ". . . SHE WAS OFF": Annie Nathan Meyer requoted by Lewis, p. 129.

p. 39 ". . . I'LL GIVE IT BACK": Zora Neale Hurston quoted by Langston Hughes, p. 378.

p. 39 "EVERYBODY DRANK TOO MUCH": Dorothy West quoted by Lorraine Elena Roses, "Dorothy West at Oak Bluffs, Massachusetts, July 1984": *Sage: A Scholarly Journal on Black Women*, 2:1 (Spring 1985): 49.

p. 39 "AN ORIGINAL": Arna Bontemps to Hemenway, p. 70.

p. 39 ". . . GENTLE EYES": Claude McKay requoted by Rampersad, p. 53.

p. 40 ". . . WENT BY MY SMALLNESS": Dorothy West quoted by Roses, p. 48.

p. 40 BANGLES AND BEADS: Hemenway, p. 61.

p. 40 DAY-CARE CENTERS: Marianna W. Davis, ed., *Contributions of Black Women to America*, Volume 1, p. viii.

p. 40 DOMESTIC JOBS: Mabel Smythe, ed., *The Black American Reference Book*, p. 1348.

p. 40 READ OR WRITE: Davis, p. 237.

p. 40 CHURCH MAGAZINES: *Ibid*, p. 237.

p. 40–41 ". . . NO RESPECTABLE JOB": Dorothy West quoted by Roses, p. 48.

p. 42 "UNTAINTED": Lewis, p. 95.

p. 44 QUICK-TEMPERED AND ARROGANT: Darwin Turner, *In a Minor Chord*, p. 98.

p. 44 "INSIGNIFICANT": Chidi Ikonne, *From Du Bois to Van Vechten*, p. 183.

p. 44 "GRAND STORYTELLER": Louise Thompson to Hemenway, p. 182.

Chapter 5. HARLEM II

p. 51 MOST AMUSING MEMBER: Langston Hughes requoted by Robert Hemenway, *Zora Neale Hurston*, p. 64. OVER FIFTY THOUSAND DOLLARS: *Ibid.*, p. 105. "GODMOTHER": *Ibid.*, p. 107. AT HER FEET: *Ibid.*, p. 107.

p. 53 ONE HUNDRED FIFTY DOLLARS A MONTH: Rampersad, p. 157.

p. 53 ". . . BROMO-SELTZER": Rampersad, p. 163. ". . . AND IN COLLEGE": Mrs. Charlotte Mason requoted *Ibid.*, p. 172.

p. 53 FIFTEEN THOUSAND DOLLARS: Hemenway, p. 105.

p. 53 TWO HUNDRED DOLLARS A MONTH: Rampersad, p. 157.

p. 53 ". . . DO SOMETHING ABOUT IT": Zora Neale Hurston requoted by Mary Helen Washington, "A Woman Half in Shadow," Introduction to *I Love Myself When I Am Laughing and Then Again When I Am Looking Mean and Impressive*, p. 13.

p. 53 "THE DIRTY WORDS": Zora Neale Hurston requoted by Hemenway, p. 129.

p. 55–56 MULE BONE: The account of the *Mule Bone* incident is based on Hemenway, Chapter Six.

p. 56 "PERFECT DARKIE": Langston Hughes, *The Langston Hughes Reader*, p. 378.

p. 56 "EXTRAVAGANT FLATTERY": David Levering Lewis, *When Harlem Was in Vogue*, p. 96. ". . . TO FIND RECOGNITION": *Ibid.*, p. 96.

p. 56 USED FLATTERY: Rampersad, p. 110.

Chapter 6. FLORIDA

p. 60   KNOWN AS ORIGINALITY: requoted by Robert Hemenway, "Florida Field Notes from Zora Neale Hurston," *Black Scholar* 7:7 (April 1976): 41.

p. 64   ". . . KNEW AS A CHILD": Zora Neale Hurston requoted by Robert Hemenway, *Zora Neale Hurston*, p. 215.

Chapter 7. NEW ORLEANS

p. 71   . . . AFRICAN TRIBES: Kyle Kristos, *Voodoo*, p. 14.

p. 72   FOUR MILLION IN HAITI: Nancy Cooper and Ron Moreau, "Haiti's Voodoo Witch Hunt," *Newsweek* 107:21 (26 May 1986): 43.

Chapter 9. HAITI

p. 83   . . . POISONED: Robert Hemenway, *Zora Neale Hurston*, p. 248.

p. 89–90   . . . FURTHER RESEARCH: Wade Davis, *The Serpent and the Rainbow*, p. 211–15. ZOMBIE POWDER: *Ibid.*, p. 226. "ZOMBIE CUCUMBER": *Ibid.*, 227.

p. 90   HAITIAN'S GREATEST FEAR: *Ibid.*, 226.

Chapter 10. NEW YORK

p. 92   ". . . PART OF BLACK LIFE": Mary Helen Washington requoted by Rita Dandridge in *But Some of Us Are Brave*, p. 274.

Chapter 11. DUST TRACKS

p. 99   "MINSTREL IMAGE": Richard Wright, "Between Laughter and Tears," *New Masses*, 5 October: 22.

p. 99   ". . . NOTHING ELSE": Richard Wright requoted by Robert Hemenway, *Zora Neale Hurston*, p. 335.

p. 99   ". . . MACHINE-GUN FIRE": Zora Neale Hurston to Ralph Hartman, 26 April 1940, Beaufort, South Carolina.

p. 100   FIVE THOUSAND COPIES: Hemenway, *Zora Neale Hurston*, p. 6.

p. 100   ". . . LIFE IN AMERICA": Arna Bontemps, "From
            Eatonville, Florida, to Harlem: Zora Hurston Always
            Had What It Takes, and Lots of It," *New York Herald
            Tribune Books*, 22 November: 3.

p. 100   RECYCLING FOLK MATERIAL: Edward W. Farrison,
            Review of *Dust Tracks on a Road*. *Journal of Negro
            History*, 28:3 (July 1943): 6.

p. 100   ". . . GIFTED MIND": Hemenway, *Zora Neale
            Hurston*, p. 289.

p. 100   ATTEND THE PROM: Hemenway, Introduction to
            Dust Tracks on a Road, p. xiii.

p. 101   "PUBLISHERS INSISTED": Zora Neale Hurston to
            Ralph Hartman, 10 January 1943, Daytona Beach,
            Florida.

p. 101   "SUPERB WORK": Gordon E. Bigelow and Laura V.
            Monti, *The Selected Letters of Marjorie Kinnan Raw-
            lings*, p. 223. "AS A HUMAN BEING AND A FRIEND":
            Ibid., p. 223. FONDNESS FOR ZORA: *Ibid.*, p. 293.
            ". . . KIND TO EVERYBODY": *Ibid.*, p. 313.

p. 102   CAPABLE OF LEARNING: Zora Neale Hurston re-
            quoted by Al Hurt, "Zora Neale Hurston: Florida's
            Forgotten Daughter," *The Miami Herald* (Sunday, 22
            August 1976), sec. G, p. 6.

p. 102   ". . . SEGREGATION MESS": *Ibid.*

p. 102   ". . . ALL MY LIFE": requoted by Fannie Hurst,
            "Zora Hurston: A Personality Sketch," *The Yale Uni-
            versity Library Gazette*, 35 (1961): 20.

Chapter 12. FLORIDA

p. 107   ". . . KICK THE BUCKET": Zora Neale Hurston re-
            quoted by Robert Hemenway, *Zora Neale Hurston*,
            p. 302.

p. 108   "ANTI-NEGRO": *Ibid.*, p. 319.

p. 108   "UPPITY": Lorraine Bethel, "This Infinity of Con-
            scious Pain," *But Some of Us Are Brave*, p. 185.

p. 109   ". . . WITHOUT REASON": Zora Neale Hurston re-
            quoted by Robert Hemenway, *Zora Neale Hurston*,
            p. 321.

p. 109   ". . . LOOKED TO AND CHERISHED": *Ibid.*, p. 32. "AWE AND TERROR": *Ibid.*, p. 305.

p. 110   ". . . GOOD FOR EVERYONE": *Ibid.*, p. 325. ". . . HERE AND THERE": *Ibid.*, p. 338. "WORLD'S MOST BEAUTIFUL RIVER": *Ibid.*, p. 340.

p. 111   WRITER FOR THE PAPER: Telephone conversation between C. E. Bolen and Mary Lyons, 13 May 1989.

p. 111   HOROSCOPES: *Ibid.*, and Alice Walker, "Looking for Zora," *In Search of Our Mothers' Gardens*, p. 112.

p. 111   "LIVE ROUGHLY": C. E. Bolen to Mary Lyons. ". . . IN HER BRAIN": *Ibid.*

p. 111   ". . . WITH THOSE WORDS": C. E. Bolen quoted by Al Hurt, "Zora Neale Hurston: Florida's Forgotten Daughter," *The Miami Herald* (Sunday, 22 August 1976), sec. G, p. 6.

p. 111   ". . . SHE WAS JUST DIFFERENT": Margaret Paige, *Ibid.*

p. 112   ". . . MILK COW": Zora Neale Hurston to Ralph Hartman, 18 May 1939, Jacksonville, Florida.

p. 112 $18 RENT: Zora Neale Hurston, dust jacket from *Seraph on the Suwanee*.

p. 112 $943.75: Alice Walker, Introduction to Hemenway's *Zora Neale Hurston*, p. 5.

p. 113   LOCAL JAM SESSIONS: Telephone conversation between A. E. Backus and Mary Lyons, 9 August 1989.

p. 113   ". . . CRY THE NEXT": Langston Hughes, *The Langston Hughes Reader*, p. 378.

p. 113   ". . . SEE 'BOUT ME": requoted by Alice Walker, "Looking for Zora," *In Search of Our Mothers' Gardens*, p. 111. ". . . WORKED ALL THE TIME": *Ibid.*

p. 113   ". . . GET HER DOWN": A. E. Backus to Mary Lyons.

p. 113   ". . . TO GET BETTER": *Ibid.*

p. 113   "$600: "Final Rites Sunday for Author Zora Neale Hurston at Peek's," *Fort Pierce Chronicle* (Friday, 12 February 1960).

p. 113   PALLBEARERS: *Ibid.*

p. 114   BRONZE METALLIC CASKET: *Ibid.*

p. 118   FLOWERS IN HER MEMORY: Bernie Woodall, "Graveside Memorial for Black Author," *Fort Pierce News Tribune* (Wednesday, 3 April 1985).

p. 120   YOUNGER THAN SHE: Hemenway, p. 273 (Zora's second husband, Albert Price, was twenty-three. Counting the ten "lost years" of her life, she was forty-eight.)

p. 120   ". . . AFRAID AGAIN": Zora Neale Hurston to Ralph Hartman, 7 October 1940, New York City.

p. 120   ". . . WAS AN ESKIMO": Bruce Nugent requoted by Hemenway, p. 70.

Author's Note

p. 124   ". . . SAVE A FIGHT": Zora Neale Hurston, "Georgia Skin," field recording in Library of Congress, Archive of Folk Song (Accession numbers 309–535).

SUGGESTED READING

Faulkner, William J. *The Days When the Animals Talked*. Chicago: Follett, 1977.

Hamilton, Virginia. *The People Could Fly*. New York: Knopf, 1985.

Harris, Joel Chandler. *Jump! The Adventures of Brer Rabbit*. Adapted by Van Dyke Parks. New York: Harcourt Brace Jovanovich, 1986.

———. *Jump Again! More Adventures of Brer Rabbit*. Adapted by Van Dyke Parks. New York: Harcourt Brace Jovanovich, 1987.

Hurston, Zora Neale. *Moses, Man of the Mountain*. Chicago: University of Illinois, 1984. Reprint of the edition published by J. B. Lippincott, Philadelphia, 1939.

———. *Mules and Men*. Bloomington: Indiana University Press, 1978. Reprint of the edition published by J. B. Lippincott, Philadelphia, 1935.

Kristos, Kyle. *Voodoo*. New York: J. B. Lippincott, 1976.

Lester, Julius. *Black Folktales*. New York: Grove Press, 1969.

———. *More Tales of Uncle Remus: Further Adventures of Brer Rabbit, His Friends, Enemies, and Others*. New York: Dial Press, 1988.

———. *The Tales of Uncle Remus: The Adventures of Brer Rabbit*. New York: Dial Press, 1987.

Sanfield, Steve. *The Adventures of High John the Conqueror*. New York: Orchard Books, 1989.

BIBLIOGRAPHY

Bergman, Peter M. *The Chronological History of the Negro in America*. New York: Harper & Row, 1969.

Bigelow, Gordon E., and Laura V. Monti, eds. *The Selected Letters of Marjorie Kinnan Rawlings*. Gainsville, Fla.: University Press of Florida, 1983.

Davis, Arthur P. *From the Dark Tower*. New York: Howard University Press, 1974.

Davis, Marianna W., ed. *Contributions of Black Women to America*. Vol. 1–2. Columbia, S.C.: Kenday Press, 1982.

Davis, Wade. *The Serpent and the Rainbow*. New York: Simon and Schuster, 1985.

Hemenway, Robert. Introduction to *Dust Tracks on a Road*. Chicago: University of Illinois Press, 1984.

———. *Zora Neale Hurston: A Literary Biography*. Chicago: University of Illinois Press, 1977.

Hughes, Langston. *The Langston Hughes Reader*. New York: George Braziller, 1958.

Hull, Gloria, Patricia Scott, and Barbara Smith, eds. *But Some of Us Are Brave*. New York: The Feminist Press, 1982.

Hurston, Zora Neale. *Dust Tracks on a Road*. New York: J. B. Lippincott, 1942.

————. "High John de Conquer." *The American Mercury Reader*. Philadelphia: The Blakiston Co., 1944.

————. *Jonah's Gourd Vine*. Philadelphia: J. B. Lippincott, 1934.

————. *Mules and Men*. Philadelphia: J. B. Lippincott, 1935.

————. *Tell My Horse*. Philadelphia: J. B. Lippincott, 1938.

————. *Their Eyes Were Watching God*. Philadelphia: J. B. Lippincott, 1937.

————. "Zora Neale Hurston Writes About Herself": Dust jacket from *Seraph on the Suwanee*. New York: Charles Scribner's Sons, 1948.

Ikonne, Chidi. *From Du Bois to Van Vechten*. Westport, Conn.: Greenwood Press, 1981.

Kristos, Kyle. *Voodoo*. Philadelphia: J. B. Lippincott Co., 1976.

Kunitz, Stanley J., ed. *Twentieth-Century American Authors*. New York: H. W. Wilson Co., 1942.

Lewis, David Levering. *When Harlem Was in Vogue*. New York: Random House, 1982.

Locke, Alain, ed. *The New Negro: An Interpretation*. New York: A. C. Boni, 1925.

Low, Augustus, and Virgil Clift. *Encyclopedia of Black America*. New York: McGraw-Hill, 1981.

Meier, August, and Elliott Rudwick. *From Plantation to Ghetto*. New York: Hill and Wang, 1970.

Newson, Adele S. *Zora Neale Hurston: A Reference Guide*. Boston: G. K. Hall, 1987.

Rampersad, Arnold. *The Life of Langston Hughes*. Vol. 1, 1902–1941: *I, Too, Sing America*. New York: Oxford University Press, 1986.

Smythe, Mabel M. *The Black American Reference Book*. Englewood Cliffs, N.J.: Prentice-Hall, 1976.

Turner, Darwin. *In a Minor Chord: Three Afro-American Writers and Their Search for Identity*. Carbondale, Ill.: Southern Illinois University Press, 1971.

Walker, Alice, ed. *I Love Myself When I Am Laughing and Then Again When I Am Looking Mean and Impressive*. New York: The Feminist Press, 1979.

Walker, Alice. *In Search of Our Mothers' Gardens*. New York: Harcourt Brace Jovanovich, 1983.

Washington, Mary Helen. "Zora Neale Hurston: A Woman Half in Shadow." Introduction to *I Love Myself When I Am Laughing and Then Again When I Am Looking Mean and Impressive: A Zora Neale Hurston Reader*. Old Westbury, N.Y.: Feminist Press, 1979.

Wesley, Charles, ed. *International Library of Afro-American Life and History: The Quest for Equality from Civil War to Civil Rights*. Cornwell Heights, Pa.: The Association for the Study of Afro-American Life and History, 1978.

Wright, Gwendolyn. *Building the Dream: A Social History of Housing in America*. New York: Pantheon Books, 1981.

INDEX